ALL IS WELL

ALL IS WELL

YOU ARE EXACTLY WHERE YOU'RE MEANT TO BE

ERICA KORMAN

Copyright © 2023 Erica Korman
All rights reserved.

ALL IS WELL
You Are Exactly Where You're Meant to Be

FIRST EDITION

ISBN   978-1-5445-3719-1   Paperback
       978-1-5445-3720-7   Ebook

*This book is first dedicated to my mom and dad,
whom my soul chose as parents to teach me all of the very
difficult and beautiful lessons I needed to learn in this
lifetime to heal myself and others. My mom guides
me from heaven and my dad from earth.*

*Second, I dedicate this book to my daughters,
Chloe and Lola, the two coolest humans
I've truly ever met. I'm in awe of you both daily and
could write a whole book about each of you individually
as there are no words to express how honored I am to
be your mama. We've had many, many lifetimes together
(even if you doubt that!) and to get to play this "role"
as your mom in this one is the best gift ever!
Don't forget to follow your intuition always, follow your
passions, and live the magical life of your dreams, always!
I support you in all you choose to be and am
so proud of each of you every day and love you
more than I can express in words.*

—Erica/Mommy

CONTENTS

Introduction | 1

LESSON ONE
The Dead Don't Care
(They Just Want You to Be Okay) | 13

LESSON TWO
Everything Happens According
to Divine Timing of the Universe | 33

LESSON THREE
What's Calling You Is Your Purpose | 47

LESSON FOUR
Helping Others Helps *You* | 61

LESSON FIVE
Grounding Is Everything | 77

LESSON SIX

Boundaries = Safety for Everyone | 97

LESSON SEVEN

Always Keep Growing and Healing | 117

LESSON EIGHT

Self-Love Is the Answer | 129

Conclusion | 135

Acknowledgments | 139

INTRODUCTION

If there's one thing I want you to take away from everything I'm about to tell you, it's that "all is well."

No, wait. It's so much more than that. All is better than well—it's magical. Beyond magical! And you are *always* exactly where you're meant to be.

That is the biggest bullshit I've ever heard, you might be saying to yourself. *My life doesn't feel magical at all right now. It's not a dream; it's a total nightmare.*

If you're going through a divorce, struggling with your mental health, managing sickness or injuries, coping with the loss of a loved one, or dealing with any other difficult circumstances, hear me out before you throw this book across the room and never read another page. Believe me, I've experienced some difficult shit in my life. Like you, I continue to have my fair share of lessons to be learned in my healing process. Yet I *still* believe all is magical.

How? Not to mention, why?

Because after speaking to thousands of people who have passed over, this has been reiterated to me time and again: we all choose our path in life before we're born. We actually sign up for the lessons our souls need to learn, which are all in service of our soul's growth. It all makes perfect sense.

Now you may be thinking, *Wait a minute. So you're saying I asked for all this? I wouldn't wish this on my worst enemy!* Although I hear you (I felt the same), the truth of the matter is, yes, you did. And so did I, even though I can't imagine agreeing to lose my mother at seventeen or to go through the other traumas and losses I've experienced. They were painful beyond belief and almost destroyed me, but they also taught me everything I needed to grow, learn, and live out my purpose here on earth.

What can I tell you? This is just how the Universe works. Back in the spiritual world—our true home—we all pick our parents, our life's course, and our death. Our souls make contracts with everyone we'll meet, for good and for bad. We reincarnate with the same "soul family" (a very close group of souls who share many, many lifetimes together) over and over again to help each other grow as souls. We create our lives like a play, bringing in the actors necessary to enact the script. Of course, we don't remember all this once we get to earth—our soul's school—because it must be forgotten to learn our lessons in life.

Since we don't get to choose exactly how these will be learned (the Universe takes care of that), things don't always go the way we expect, want, or hope while we're here. We have specific lessons to learn, but the way we learn them is determined once we're here and we also have "free will" to change the plot a bit as we are advancing on our soul's journey. Still, we can take comfort in knowing we're always exactly where we're meant to be, even when we don't like where that is.

Especially when we don't like where that is.

THE UNIVERSE IS YOUR BESTIE

Now for some good news: you don't need to stay where you are right now if you don't want to. You're in control of your own actions. You always have free will. Things can even shift in the script you created back in the spiritual world depending on how quickly you learn your soul's lessons and what's happening on the planet during your lifetime.

Just know that throughout it all, the Universe is your bestie and always on your side—you just need to stop fighting it and start working with it. Leaning into my spiritual side is the best way

I've found to partner with the Universe. The upcoming chapters of this book offer a variety of ways you can do that, too.

For now, though, I want to start our journey together by asking you to get in touch with your truest emotions, dreams, and desires. Sit in your feelings. Allow yourself to really feel them. Invite it all in and accept it.

If something difficult comes up, try to remember that pain is fluid—it moves through you and will flow away eventually. The more you resist, the more it persists. The more you allow it in and surrender to it, the more it flows. That's just the Universe working with us to invite healing and growth. We need to "feel it to heal it."

We live in a society that has always told us—especially men—not to express our emotions, so a lot of us don't even know where to start here. We're so afraid of the unknown and of losing control that we shove everything down and pretend it doesn't exist. Too bad that's just piling shit on top of more shit. It's such a human reaction to be like, *Oh fuck, I don't want to feel this way, so I'm going to take something to change that*, but numbing out on alcohol or drugs, overexercising, under- or overeating, or having too much plastic surgery or sex for the wrong reasons are "quick fixes." Unfortunately, they never really fix the pain inside. Running away from your problems or the places you're stuck in life doesn't work. Trust me, I've been there.

The fact that you picked up this book says to me you're ready to start working with the Universe to come to terms with your life and figure out where you want to go next, so consider this your challenge to do just that. Once the energy and emotions have passed through you, you'll be ready to graduate and move to the next level. To go be who and what you were born to be. To live the life you've always dreamed of but never fully believed could come true.

There is a natural flow to life when we get in alignment with our true selves. What once was hard becomes effortless. Everything starts to make sense and fall into place. The Universe presents us with the next steps we have to take. We are always being guided; we just need to get quiet and "tune in" and trust this inner guidance.

Think of where you are now as a tunnel, and know the only way out is through. Have faith; there is light up ahead.

FIND YOUR PURPOSE

We're all born for a purpose. We are here to learn lessons for our soul's growth and follow what lights us up and makes us feel good. A passion and gifts that make life worth living are bestowed on every single one of us. The adventure and purpose of life is in finding out what those are.

I always knew my passion and gift was helping others ease and heal their pain. The only thing I ever questioned was how? How was I going to be the biggest help to the most people?

In my early twenties, after getting my undergrad degree in psychology, I continued my graduate and postgrad education in psychodynamic psychotherapy at NYU to become a psychotherapist. I worked with all kinds of people: drug addicts, murderers, rapists, alcoholics, schizophrenics, sexually and physically abused children, incarcerated men, you name it. Whatever the issue, I saw my patients' struggle and held space for their pain. It was intense.

But I always sensed I could be doing more. That there was a different way to help people heal and "feel better" quicker.

My impression as a therapist (and also as someone who participated in traditional therapy for years myself) is that it moves agonizingly slowly for most people. Talking about difficult events over and over can be more retraumatizing than healing. And no one ever seems to actually "graduate" from therapy, anyway —they either quit without resolving their issues, or they do it forever and receive "short-term" relief.

I just *knew* there had to be a different way to actually "heal" myself and others, but I didn't know what. Magically, through a series of weird (and at the time, really disturbing) events, I found out how I could actually best help people in this life. It turns out, my real gift is connecting with spirit. It's true—I'm a spiritual healer, and I can talk to the dead as well as angels and spirit guides. They are my friends, and I love them all.

It was hard for me to accept my gifts at first, but as I was trying to deny my gifts and their power, I was receiving lifesaving information. Eventually, I couldn't ignore it.

One time (in the very beginning), I clearly saw a picture of a friend in my head and kept hearing the numbers *six, two, six, three* repeated. Somehow, I knew I was supposed to call her. When she picked up the phone, I asked, "What does six, two, six, three mean to you?" She started freaking out and told me, "Literally, I just hung up the phone with my sister. She was saying that our dead father was six foot three, and I was saying he was six two."

Just then, something more came to me. I told her, "I'm so sorry, but this is a really strong message. Your dad wants you to go have a breast examination." At the time, we were pretty young, and mammograms weren't even recommended for us yet. Still, she agreed to see a doctor. It turns out, her doctor said she had a growth in her breast that could have become cancer. She had it removed and is fine now. What her dad told me to tell her possibly saved her life!

After practicing mediumship for a while, I discovered I had other healing abilities as well. I learned I was able to heal people with my hands, moving dis-ease—toxic, stuck, negative energy—out of their bodies and replacing it with clean, positive, light energy. Whenever I practiced this, people started feeling better, and their symptoms—the headaches, chest pains, and dizziness—began to go away. This was more magic!

I kept going, learning and obsessively studying everything I could about chakras, which are the energy centers in the body. Now I am able to read and cleanse these centers, removing energy that needs to be released so the body becomes healthier and lighter and flows better.

Being a psychic medium and spiritual healer helps people in a whole different way than traditional therapy. It gets to the core of the issues with a lightness and is so beautiful, instead of everything being so heavy and dense all the time. Imagine hearing that your dead grandma sees how you're neglecting yourself and really wants you to take care of your health and ways that you can do that and validation that she's always with you and so much more. This is magical healing on another level. My intention isn't to negate or insult traditional therapy, as everyone needs to do what's right for them. For me, after wearing both hats and being a participant in both, I'm blown away at how much more quickly healing happens when it's spiritually driven. There's nothing better than that—to feel better quicker. The new world we are living in is fortunately "waking up" to this work and seeking it out after trying other methods that didn't work for them. Many of my clients are in the public eye or high profile, and they always say they've tried everything and spent so much to heal and feel better and the spiritual way felt the most "right" to them. This of course includes many other healing modalities, not just mediumship.

Even though I was super freaked out and tried to push them away when I first found out about my abilities, over time I've come to a place of utter gratitude, awe, and deep love for them. I feel honored to do this work. It's very intense, but whether I'm giving clients messages from people who have passed, providing spiritual guidance, cleaning and balancing their energy systems, or just connecting with the Universe, it's beyond beautiful and feels like magic to me! I am so grateful to be able to do this work, and it's a fulfilling, magical feeling knowing I'm finally living my true purpose and passion.

If you haven't quite figured out what yours is yet, my guess is the only thing holding you back is fear. I want you to know it's okay to be afraid and to struggle. There's a reason—*your* reason and purpose—that will make it all worth it in the end. Keep going. Whenever you're ready to go beyond fear, I will be right here waiting for you.

BELIEVE IN MAGIC

Like I said, I want to help as many people as I can in this life, and I'm excited about that. But for the people I can't connect with directly, I wanted to find a way to share what recovering from my past trauma and becoming a spiritual healer has taught me. This book is that way.

Spirit—you might call it the Universe, Divine, God, or something else entirely—has revealed so much to me, and now I get to pass that information on to you. Every chapter of this book contains a big lesson I learned, the way it manifested in my life, and how you can use that knowledge to light your path forward. I'm not saying it will solve all your problems, but it *will* help you start to explore why you're here, what to do with that information, and how to focus on your healing. There's something bigger and better in life for you, and you can still live the life of your dreams!

Whether you are currently struggling or simply on your way toward a spiritual awakening, my biggest wish is that you find peace, comfort, and guidance in this book. Even though I talk about some difficult things in these pages, always remember the messages I'm bringing you are based on love and light. This story is literally my journey from the darkness into light, and I'm honored and humbled to share it with you.

Everything is exactly as it's meant to be. All is well. All is magical.

Make that beyond magical!

LESSON ONE

The Dead Don't Care (They Just Want You to Be Okay)

One night just before she died, my mom was annoying me about studying for my SATs. Being a hormonal and angry sixteen-year-old, I screamed at her, "Leave me alone. I wish you were dead!" and stormed out of the room. I was just so angry that she was sick and going to leave me soon. We were always close and usually got along great, so of course she accepted my apology and everything was fine between us after that. But until I was aware that I was able to connect with her from the other side, I always regretted those words so much. Since being in touch with my dead mother daily as a medium and talking to so many others as well, I've learned our loved ones do not care about the stuff we worry about on this dense physical plane we call earth. They are in a world of love, light, and peace—Heaven. They are learning, too, but our superficial matters don't mean anything to them.

I grew up in an upper-middle-class town that was quintessential, idyllic suburbia. Set on the shores of the Long Island Sound, there was a beach at the end of our block. The downtown was so quaint that it almost looked like a movie set. Add in a convenient commute into Manhattan, and it was a place everyone wanted to live. Still do.

The street where I lived was lined with traditional three-bedroom homes. Everyone's yards had freshly mown grass and colorful flowers planted out front. Backyards blended one into the next without fences to break up all that open space.

It was a safe and happy place to be raised, and my older sister and I had free rein over it all. We spent our days together making mini bouquets with dandelions and wild daisies to use in our Barbie doll weddings. Sometimes we'd try to get Strawberry Shortcake and my cat, Pepper, to be the bridesmaids.

We'd play with our neighborhood pals—one is still one of my best friends to this day—while our moms sat in aluminum lawn chairs, keeping an eye on us while they chatted and smoked cigarettes. I remember my mother always being close by, a beautiful presence who was never intrusive. She made me feel so confident about myself and my place in the world.

In the summer, we'd go to day camp during the week and the town pool on the weekends. I made my mom watch me perform countless submerged handstands, just like my kids when they were younger did with me, and my sister and I invented a game that basically amounted to us having an underwater tea party there. I remember playing Marco Polo with my friends until we were waterlogged and then getting a hot dog or hamburger and a popsicle at the food stand. It was a much simpler time!

When I was eight, we moved to another house across town. It was a little bit bigger and had a pool in the backyard. Now there were no more days at the public pool because I could just invite people over to swim, but mostly everything else stayed the same. I kept my friends from the old neighborhood and made some more. My dad still lives in that house today, and the names my friends and I carved into the bench at the bus stop are still there, too. Whenever I visit, I'm struck with such great nostalgia.

Throughout my childhood, my dad worked on Wall Street, so he was usually gone when I got up and didn't get home until dinnertime. In my little kid head, that meant he was never around, so of course my mom became my entire world. There was so much love between us. I used to hide underneath the covers of her bed and wait for her to come into the room, when I'd pop up and "scare" her. No matter how many times I pulled this same trick, she always acted surprised.

A teacher by profession, my mom was strong, funny, sarcastic, and not about to take any shit. Whenever she wasn't teaching ESL a few towns over, she would substitute at my school. If anyone dared mess with me or my sister, watch out. Once, my sister's friend was being mean to her and my mom told her to stop being a little bitch. Of course that friend was afraid to come over our house after that. As I write this, I realize I did exactly the same thing when one of my daughter's friends was being rude to her a few years back. I'm definitely her feisty daughter.

Mom was a smart and independent woman. She loved languages, was fluent in Spanish, and took Japanese lessons just for fun. She did needlepoint and painting, passing along her love of art to us kids. We took painting and pottery classes at an old couple's house in town, and I remember thinking what I made there was amazing. My mom always agreed with me. There's a little blue bowl I made for her still sitting by what used to be her side of the bed.

My mom looked so beautiful at my bat mitzvah, and I remember her being so proud of me for reading from the Torah in front of my friends. After the ceremony, my parents threw me a great big party, and I wore the ugliest, cheesiest dress ever. Whatever. I felt super hot and remember thinking what a great dancer I was as I did this little shimmy I'd been practicing.

Sounds like a perfect childhood, right? I thought so, too. I also thought things would stay as idyllic as they were forever.

I was only three when my mom had gotten diagnosed with late-onset Type 1 diabetes, but her health started going downhill fast in my teen years. Despite her young age, she had to go on kidney dialysis and had all sorts of complications, including heart problems.

After a while, I had no idea what she was going to be like from one day to the next. Maybe she'd be her normal self when I got home from school. Maybe she'd be asleep and not get up for the rest of the day. Maybe she'd be at the hospital. Who knew? It was a total crapshoot. One time, I asked a new friend, Lizzie, to hang out after school, and my mom stayed in bed the entire time. I was too embarrassed to have people over after that.

Little by little, all that vibrant energy she used to have left her. One of her best friends, Betty Brumer (she was a saint and still is

—thank you, Betty), would take her to dialysis and then rush to the bus stop to pick up her own kids along with me and my sister. I can never thank her enough for being there for us during those super hard times.

Through it all, my dad kept working as much—and maybe even more—than ever. He was a great provider and trying to advance in his career, but I also think work was his escape from the reality at home. By this point, my sister had zero interest in hanging out with me; she had her own friends and life that didn't have room for a little sister tagging along in it anymore. As a result, there was no one I felt comfortable talking to about the situation at home. I wasn't in any sort of therapy at the time, so negative thoughts about how I wasn't "normal" like everyone else set in. After feeling loved throughout my earlier childhood, I now felt like I was totally on my own.

When no one else stepped up to the plate to guide me through this messy and painful new reality, I realized I was simply going to have to take care of myself going forward. I eventually decided the best way to do that was by pretending to be perfect. I'm an empath, meaning I feel everyone's emotions as my own, and I just wanted to ensure everyone else was okay even if that was at the expense of my needs. They call therapists "the wounded healers," and I'd venture to say these difficult early experiences made me the classic example of that.

As much as I hoped pretending to be the perfect child who needed nothing at all would make everything okay, it of course didn't. Soon, I began to feel with absolute certainty that my mom was going to die soon (didn't realize then how intuitive I was). The doctors told us she had a chronic illness but not a terminal one, but my not-yet-discovered psychic abilities told me differently. The thought of losing my mother made me so depressed that I stopped eating. If she was going to die, I wanted to die with her.

My parents noticed I was losing weight, which I of course liked. I was also getting a lot more attention from guys and people than usual, which just made me want to do it more. Controlling my food intake became my thing.

Eventually, though, even that excitement wore off. I was always hungry and miserable. All I could think about was my mom dying, and I couldn't imagine life without her. I didn't *want* to imagine life without her.

It came to a point where I couldn't take making myself invisible in an attempt to just be seen anymore. The fear, depression, need to be perfect, and starving myself all the time just got too overwhelming. I have such compassion for the lost, sad little girl I was back then and the exercise in futility she created in her life in an attempt to stop the inevitable.

Everything felt so out of control that I told my parents I was being bullied by some mean girls at school. My statement certainly had some truth to it: There *were* mean girls at school, but I wasn't really being bullied by them. I just needed my parents to see how much I was hurting. I even admitted that sometimes I wanted to hurt myself.

My mom and dad immediately took me to see a psychiatrist in town, who agreed I was in actual trouble. My eating disorder and depression were out of hand. I was having suicidal ideations, which even if I had no immediate plans to act upon, was not okay. I was admitted to the child psychiatric ward at the local hospital.

I remember going to the fridge there one night and devouring an entire cake. It made me feel buzzed. Sick. Awesome. Mad. Sad. So many emotions I'd been pretending not to have—perfect people don't get mad or sad, right?—all at the same time. I'm sure the staff saw me because there were cameras everywhere, but they didn't stop me. Maybe they just wanted me to start eating again, even if my choice wasn't exactly healthy.

After a few days, I got transferred to another psychiatric facility in Queens, New York that was specifically for teens. As soon as I stepped foot in the place, I knew I'd made a huge mistake by practically begging my parents to take me to the hospital. The other patients there were really struggling with severe mental illness and many had already been there for months. Some maybe even closer to a year.

Now this lost, lonely little girl from Long Island was stuck in Queens, surrounded by people who had problems that seemed more complex than mine. My roommate kept talking to herself, blurting out things that were totally unrelated and inappropriate. The guy down the hall was always making sexual threats and screaming. He had no impulse control—it was like he either wanted to fuck or kill somebody all the time.

The only good part about it was the therapists. They were smart, supportive, and seemed like they had it all together. To hormonal sixteen-year-old me, they were also kind of hot. Two of the ones I liked best were dating, and I imagined their life was so cool. Plus, they were really helping people, which only made them cooler to me. I wanted to be just like them, so much so that ten years later, I was doing the same kind of work in the same kind of place. I took the pain I felt as a teen and used it to better understand and help others in the same position I was once in.

My days in the hospital were full of therapeutic interventions: talk therapy, movement therapy, and arts therapy. Movement was basically like gym in school—maybe we'd play basketball or kickball. Art was painting, drawing, or making collages from magazines. In group therapy, they'd always ask us, *How are you feeling today?* and everyone would share their deepest thoughts and fears.

I always stayed quiet because I was too scared to say anything. I guess I didn't think anyone really cared what I had to say. I realize now that my throat chakra was blocked in those years, but all I knew about it back then was that I always had a sore throat, got strep regularly, and was so shy I could never speak up for myself.

The only person I really talked to at the hospital was a skinny little rat-faced boy with a bowl cut named Matt. He was there for drug issues and depression and was nothing at all like what I'm attracted to these days. But he liked me, and I liked the attention he gave me, so we decided to be boyfriend-girlfriend.

One day in group therapy, they asked one particular girl what she was grateful for that day. I was terrified of her because she was in a gang and had a crush on Adam. She replied, "I'm grateful that Erica is going to get the hell out of here soon." She thought she and Matt would get together once I was gone, so after group therapy, she told me she was going to hurt me unless I left. She didn't have to tell me twice.

I'd never had any therapy or medication before this—I didn't even know it was an option—but especially now that the Zoloft the doctors put me on started to kick in, I was like, *Get me the fuck out of here.* I instinctively knew how to work with the psychiatrist to make that happen and was out in less than two weeks. I could already see what the system was. The sad part of all, though, was I felt more taken care of at the hospital than I did at home. Many people are unaware that we manifest physical and mental illnesses because we so desperately need to be taken care of.

I wasn't ready to deal with the outside world yet, so I didn't go straight back to school after my release from the hospital. I still wasn't feeling great and was embarrassed about the reason for my absence. I had no idea what everyone had been told, and I wasn't about to share why I'd been gone so long or where I'd been. I just wanted to be with my mom, snuggle up in bed, and hang out with her. I guess my soul knew I wouldn't have her for much longer.

My teachers delivered homework to me and then came back to collect it instead of me going to school. My art teacher was especially kind to me. We would just sit in my backyard studying or painting together. He was so calm and sweet and present with me—truly an angel. What a different slower-paced time it was then for him to be able to do this.

I went to visit Matt a few times after we got out of the hospital. He was nice, but we figured out pretty quickly the only thing we had in common was thinking the other was cute in a difficult situation. Of course our relationship didn't last. A million years later, I found a charm from a necklace he gave me in my old bedroom. Even though being in the psych ward represented a big loss of innocence for me, the brief relationship Matt and I had there was really innocent and pure.

I completed my junior year of high school at home. I really could have used someone to talk to about everything that was happening in my life, but I couldn't imagine who might welcome my painful unexpressed emotions. My sister was busy and away at college. My parents didn't have the capacity to deal with anything other than what was already on their plates. I believed my friends couldn't possibly understand because their moms were healthy and vibrant, and to my knowledge, none of them had an eating disorder or depression. Looking back, I'm sure they would have been happy to listen to and support me, but I never gave them the chance. I always said no when they invited me out. Doing all the typical teenage stuff felt meaningless to me, and I didn't want to miss any time with my mom.

It was recommended that I continue therapy after I got out of the hospital, but no one pursued that option for me, and I certainly didn't ask for it either. I just went back to acting like the perfect kid again, and my parents assumed I was fine. We were all doing the best we could, you know?

Meanwhile, my mom kept getting sicker. She didn't want to give up her ESL job, but even though it was only a few towns over, she was so exhausted that she had to pull her car over to rest those last few times she went. That was heartbreaking for her, and for me, too. I hated watching my strong, resilient mother fading away like that.

Then came a day I'll never forget, as much I wish I could. I was sitting at the kitchen table wearing a tight red, orange, and yellow Esprit shirt—the coolest brand at the time—and light blue super-short cutoff jean shorts. I had just put a frozen pizza in the oven for my dinner and was getting ready to watch *Dallas* on my tiny white bubble TV (very popular at the time) when my father walked in with my aunt. They had just come home from the hospital, and I knew exactly what had happened. I saw their faces and wanted to stop time. I had just seen my mother the day before, but now Mommy was gone. My whole world crashed down around me.

I knew logically that my mom didn't die because of the mean thing I'd said to her. But my confused and depressed teenage brain still *felt* like that's why it happened. I held on to that guilt for so, so long.

Way too long, as it turns out.

WHAT I NOW KNOW

The dead don't care about what we said or did or didn't say or do in this life. They are in a higher place that transcends our human emotions. I assure you, thousands of loved ones in spirit have expressed this to me over and over again: everything is exactly as it was meant to be. It all had to happen the way it did for everyone to learn the lessons they came here to learn. That was a big relief for me, and I hope it is for you, too.

The most common question I get as a medium is, Is my mom/dad/brother/sister/grandma/grandpa still mad/upset/disappointed in me? And the answer is always no. Of the thousands of people I've connected with who have passed on, I can honestly tell you that none of them give a shit about any of that. They don't have regrets or hold grudges like we do here on earth. It's only our crazy human brains that think that way. There is no guilt, lack, fear, anger, or any of the lower vibration emotions where they are now. Instead, it's all about peace, love, and healing.

I'm working with a client now who never had a good relationship with her mom, a drug addict who died as a result of her addiction, while her mother was alive. Now that her mom is in a better, clearer space—back in the love and light we all come from and return to—they talk and communicate with each other so well through our work. There's no more anger. No animosity. No drama. Only love. This is the magical healing I'm referring to that no traditional therapy can provide. It is so beautiful to be part of this healing experience they are having and it helps me heal as well.

The mom has apologized for a lot of things she did in life, not out of regret but from a place of knowing that's what her daughter needs to heal. She acknowledges how well her daughter is doing. My client, who never felt any support from her mom while she was still alive, is now like, "My mom is so cool and really sees me!" It is the most amazing connection and there are a lot of laughs. She has been able to forgive her mother for not being "present" in her life while she was alive. We have sessions often; they both love the healing and the connection. They are having a relationship now that she's in the spirit world that they didn't have when she was on earth.

I love how there is so much humor in my sessions with clients. "Spirit" is really light and funny. My client was trying to lose weight so she was watching her calories, and her mom came through to me and said something like, "It would help if you stopped snacking on the Lays potato chips every night." My client freaked out because she absolutely was eating potato chips every night! I love how this always happens. It's truly amazing.

And in case you're wondering, no, I'm not afraid of dead people. They are not scary and they can't harm you. Living people's energy is so heavy and dense and scary to me at times, but the energy of someone who has passed is so beautiful and light. It's hard to put that experience into words, but whenever we connect, it's always magical and healing. Spirit is all about love, light, joy, and laughter. It's so beautiful.

Most of us don't know it, but we're all channels. When a thought just pops into your head so intensely, that's from Spirit. The only difference with my experience is that I know exactly which Spirit is talking to me and who needs to hear their messages.

You know how gifted performers say ideas just come to them? That's because they're connected to the spiritual world in such an intense way that they're being channeled to share Spirit's message through their music or art. They're the vessel through which Spirit speaks, just like we all are.

These days, my mom's presence and energy pops in for me all the time. She doesn't always bring me specific messages (that mostly comes from my spirit guides), just love. We all have our own "guides in spirit" helping and guiding us in this lifetime. As for my mom, Billy Joel was her favorite, and we have developed our own communication through him. I always know it's her when a song of his comes on or I see his name somewhere, and it always seems to come at a time when I could use her guidance and support most. I love the signs. I'm sure you have them, too. Trust and believe them because they are so real.

I recently connected with my grandmother and mother at the same time through another medium friend (we do this so we can relax and not have to do all the work). They both came through very clearly. I didn't know this when they were still alive, but they were also psychic, as are my sister and cousin. I guess it's just in our genes! My mom and grandmother told me how excited they are that I am following this path, especially because they felt like they couldn't even *talk* about their abilities while they were on earth, much less use them. Lately when I'm driving, I often feel my grandmother and mother in the front seat with me, and I'm always like, *Hey guys!* I love knowing they're both here, cheering me on. I have them both here with me now as I'm writing this book outside in the Miami sun. They say right now that they are proud of me for sharing my truth.

I've also had a lot of famous people who were murdered come through to me. They are angels in Heaven, and they all want their loved ones to heal, not mourn and rage forever. Like all of us—even though it's hard to comprehend—they chose everything that happened in their lives. Our court system and the way we need to handle things here for law and order doesn't exist in the spiritual world, so they don't care who harmed them because they know karma will work itself out in the end. This is deep stuff and not something I share when someone is recently grieving their loved one. But many people find it comforting after the initial shock and grief has healed a bit.

I recently worked with a woman who lost her best friend and his five-year-old son in the Surfside, Miami building collapse a few years ago. In our session, her lost loved one sent love, support, and comfort to her. He wanted her to know he's around, watching over her, and just wants her to be okay. The son didn't really talk to me; he just bounced around like a ball of angelic love and light. Young people who pass early are such advanced souls. They have such a high vibration that it's sometimes hard to "speak" to them like I do with other souls. I see and feel their super-bright light and it feels like they are bouncing all around spreading so much love.

The bottom line here is that loved ones who have passed want you to release your guilt. *Oh, I didn't spend enough time with them at the end. I said something mean and never apologized. I wasn't there when I should have been.* None of that matters. People on the other side are doing great. They're not bored or angry or holding grudges; they're love and light and freedom. They're happy. They're able to soar and learn. They'd much rather be there than here.

The people you've loved who are now gone are all good, I promise. They want you to know how much they love you and how proud they are of you. They are at peace (some are in a deeper place of learning lessons) and want you to be at peace.

And they want you to know that they are always right there with you.

LESSON TWO

Everything Happens According to Divine Timing of the Universe

My mom died in June when I was seventeen years old.

My friends had no idea what to say to me. Some had maybe experienced a grandparent dying, but it was completely foreign to them to lose a parent. My situation made them so uncomfortable that they didn't know how to act around me anymore, and I honestly ended up feeling bad for *them*. I was picking up on their energy and could feel their sadness and pain for me, even though I didn't consciously recognize that at the time. That's what we "empaths" do.

I knew I had to get up and speak at my mom's funeral. I wrote a poem that tried to explain what she'd meant to me and how much I missed her already. Even though I was shaking, crying, and terrified, I read it in front of everyone.

My mommy has gone and no words can say
How much I wish for just one more day.
Just one more day to hold her and show
My love for her was more than anyone can know.
My mom taught me how to be so strong
No matter what, she always pushed me along…

There was more to it, but that's all I remember. Everyone was crying by the time I got to the last line. I was, too.

While I was sitting Shiva (the mourning tradition in the Jewish religion), I went completely numb, and I can see now that the trauma caused me to "dissociate." Friends and family came and went in a blur. I went through the motions and tried to act normal, but what was normal about the situation? Absolutely nothing.

After Shiva was over, everyone picked up and went back to their lives, but I found myself in a whole new reality. It was just me and my dad, and you could practically reach out and touch the sadness and emptiness in our house. As an empath, I felt my dad's loneliness almost as much as mine and tried my best to comfort him. Double the misery was not something I was equipped to deal with on my own.

I was hoping someone might volunteer to help guide me after that, but everyone was deep in their own grief, didn't know what to do, or wasn't aware of the extreme loneliness of my situation. Family and friends I expected to stick around stopped calling and visiting. I was like, *Where did everyone go?* I was so angry about it for so many years, but I've since realized they not only didn't know how to help me but probably didn't even know how to handle their own loss.

And so instead of leaning on a trusted adult or therapist to help me navigate my difficult situation, I headed off on a trip to study in Israel. I know that sounds crazy, but the trip had been planned before my mom died, and I guess my dad wanted to maintain some "normalcy" in my life. We were so lost and confused that neither of us had any idea what else to do.

What a disaster. My mom had died only three weeks before I left. I hadn't met any of the twenty other New York-area kids who were going. I was surrounded by absolute strangers. It was by no means the way to enjoy world travel.

Still, I tried to act like someone who hadn't just gone through major trauma, but I was a "numbed-out" mess. I made some friends. We toured cities. We hiked. We saw some ancient religious sites. At the Wailing Wall, there's a tradition where people write prayers on little pieces of paper and stick them into the cracks of the old stone. I wrote that I wanted my mom back. I was nasty and angry and rageful at the world and I shouldn't have been away on a trip with strangers then.

By the time I got home, I felt some relief. I didn't have to pretend to be okay anymore, and I wasn't. There was so much pain filling the air that I could barely breathe. I wandered from room to room, hoping for a sign or something from my mom. Holding the little blue bowl I'd made for her at pottery class, I curled up on her side of the bed, wishing she could still be there with me.

When that endless summer finally ended, it was time for me to go face my senior year of high school. I hadn't been back to school since the hospital, and I was nervous about how people were going to react. I felt like everyone knew why I hadn't been there for most of the second semester of junior year, and now I had a dead mother on top of my embarrassing psych ward stay.

I'm grateful I had a few great girlfriends (some of whom I'm still close with today) during this time. I was pretty much a walking zombie, but their presence and love helped me more than they'll ever know.

I was sure the other kids thought I was a freak, though, which I felt was confirmed when people who barely spoke to me went out of their way to be super nice to me. Like, way too nice. For example, this group of boys I used to be really close to (until I cheated on one of them) started talking to me again after a full year of never acknowledging my existence. I could feel the fakeness, but I had no idea how back then I was able to read and "see through" people as I call it today.

Other boys were a different story, though. That was the year I traded my eating disorder for sex. I didn't drink or smoke or anything else that would numb me out from my feelings, so sex became my drug of choice. It gave me the physical connection and attention I craved.

I lost my virginity to a guy who had been pursuing me for a while. He pretended to like me, and I was in such a low place that I ate up his advances. We had sex in my basement while my dad was at work. I wasn't regretful after, but I wasn't deliriously happy either. I didn't feel much of anything, really. Ever. Not just about sex but about everything. I found out later he'd made a bet with his friends that he could fuck me. Lovely. I was numb and lost anyway, so it didn't matter much to me.

Sleeping with him wasn't just a one-time thing, though. I hooked up with him a lot. He acted like he wanted to be my boyfriend even though I knew he was seeing another girl. I was so lost and confused that I accepted those crumbs of affection. Sometimes the sex was okay, but other times it seemed rough and scary. I figured not saying no was the same as saying yes and that I must have wanted it that way or something.

One day, my dad came home from work early and unexpectedly, found the guy in my bed, and lost his shit. My heart dropped, and I felt like such a terrible disappointment of a daughter. Dad screamed at the top of his lungs, "Get the fuck out of my house!" and the kid jumped off my second-story balcony and sprained his ankle. I was grounded, and my father and I didn't speak to each other for weeks after that.

In fact, he wouldn't even look at me. He'd order takeout ribs and fried mushrooms from the Rib Roost restaurant, and we'd eat together in silence like the other one wasn't even at the table. Everything was so tense.

While I was grounded and getting the silent treatment, I sneaked over to my hookup's house. His mom was there, and it was totally awkward because we were used to being alone at my house and doing whatever we wanted. I didn't stay long. Apparently, she told him after that I was rude because one time I didn't say hello to her at his lacrosse game or something. I had no idea she was even there, but that was a problem. So was the fact that he was seeing other girls. It was really starting to hurt my feelings.

I started thinking, *If he can see other people, then so can I.* So one day, I invited a different guy from school over to my house. He was cute, another lacrosse player I'd always liked.

We were in the basement watching TV when he forced himself on me. I was completely disassociated the whole time but made it clear I wasn't enjoying it. He seemed embarrassed and confused but didn't stop. It was definitely date rape, although I didn't have those words to put around the experience at the time.

I could tell he felt bad and weird afterward. I was so hurt and so mad that I refused to talk to him anymore. I didn't say hi to him at school. Instead, I pretended he didn't exist and only told a single friend what had happened.

When I was in my twenties, I finally got the courage to talk to that same friend about it. She was surprised I still hadn't made sense of the situation, but if you've ever wondered why women (or men) don't report these types of experiences until years later or never, it's because the trauma is so severe that we push down the memories for as long as we can. We don't want to remember or believe it happened and possibly be told that we are wrong and our trauma did not occur. That is retraumatization to a whole other level. When the memories resurface, though, watch out. That's exactly what happened to me, and it was so painful reliving that moment. I was depressed and so rageful. I felt so violated. Looking back now, I have such compassion for my younger self who had just lost her mother and was looking for love in all the wrong places. I've done such deep inner-child work to "love her up" (my coach Cristina's words) so good.

I never confronted either guy. I think at the time, I thought scraps of attention were better than nothing. Some love was better than no love. Some connection was better than no connection. It's sad to realize now, but that's just where I was. I've now forgiven myself and them both because of the intense healing work I've done around those experiences. I'm also aware that we attract where we are at in life and what we need to learn for our soul's lessons and growth, no matter how hard they are.

Senior year is supposed to be so much fun—a time to enjoy after the culmination of all that hard work in high school—but mine just wasn't turning out that way. Nothing seemed divinely timed. I wasn't going out to parties, and I couldn't muster up much interest in thinking about college. I had a dead mom and two guys I liked and trusted who had betrayed me to deal with, which made it feel impossible to enjoy the present or plan for the future. Thankfully, I did have some loyal girlfriends and a few lovely male friends who were good, respectful, and kind to me. There are always angels to be found during the tough times, and they were mine during this time.

A guidance counselor helped me apply to schools, but picking one was a joke—like choosing a random door on a game show. Everyone else was acting like this was the biggest thing in their life, but I felt like my life had stopped when my mom died. I was stuck in survival mode. In the end, I decided to go to college in Washington, DC, because I had visited the city once and thought it would be a cool place to live. I was "out of it" and didn't really care much.

Graduation was just as disappointing as everything else that year. Most kids had their entire family in the audience, but my mom was missing and I didn't have an extended tribe to cheer me on like many other kids did. I can now see that back then, I was focusing only on the lack in my life because it felt like there was so much. Today, I focus on the blessings and abundance in my life as there is so much. Like my all-time favorite spiritual teacher

Wayne Dyer says, "When you change the way you look at things, the things you look at change." That is my favorite quote of his. I do see that it's not always easy to see the world this way, but I'm grateful that through much healing and hard work on myself, I am able to have that perspective now.

I needed to find a new direction. To change my perspective. To see the goodness in the world again.

WHAT I NOW KNOW

We all choose our parents to help our souls learn the lessons we need on earth, just like we all choose our deaths and approximately when and how they'll happen. This comes along with "free will" while we're here to alter these choices a bit if needed for our soul's growth. This is a hard concept to grasp, especially when you're grieving the loss of a loved one, but I know now that my mom died once her soul learned all it needed to learn for this lifetime. She completed her purpose this time around. My father needed to lose her for their karma and his soul's journey to be complete. And I had to experience that humongous loss and pain to fulfill my purpose of being a helper and healer in this life, easing others' pain.

I chose my mom knowing her soul would only be here a short time. It was all part of the Divine plan. It took me many years of being a medium and learning from the spirit world to come to this realization. It's incredibly comforting to me to know this was all meant to happen the way it happened and that we all die right on time.

We are *always* where we're meant to be! For example, I now know I was guided to attend college in Washington, DC, to meet my future ex-husband and for other lessons in service of my soul's growth.

I used to think, w*hy me, poor me, all this shit happens to me*, but that perspective started to shift once I started learning about my gift, opening up, and becoming more spiritual. If I hadn't gone through those trials in life, I wouldn't be where I am now. I wouldn't have all the success, happiness, self-love, gratitude, and beyond abundance that exists in my life today.

Please don't get me wrong. I'm not saying you should stay in an abusive relationship or a bad situation because it's "meant to be." If you're reading this and you're in that situation, by all means, get some support and follow your guidance on what to do. Follow your inner guidance and try to learn what it came here to teach you. You now have the awareness that it isn't okay. Just know that it taught you what you needed to learn, try to release the anger and regret by feeling all your feelings and not numbing out or running from them. Try to give yourself all the love and compassion you need, and try to move forward with the help of safe people whom you trust. Look for the "earth angels"; they are always there, I promise.

Although we don't choose how we learn our lessons in life, we do have a choice in how we react to things. For example, I was with a new friend recently and started thinking, *Oh my God, she's experienced nothing. She's never been through anything difficult, so simple things seem so big to her. Life has been so easy for her.* Back then, I would have been so envious of her experiences, but now I know she has her own story in this lifetime, her own contracts and purpose to fulfill. Maybe this is her "easy" life. And that's okay. Most of us have had so many lifetimes in which we have experienced so many different identities and lessons. Who am I to judge or say what that is or how that happens?

These days, I own my story. I love my story. I love myself. I've done a ton of work with counselors, healers, and in workshops. I've read every book and watched every video on self-development I can find. I still do; I love it so much. I've studied the old-school spiritual masters and learned so much from them. I'm obsessed with this work and am always healing, learning, and growing. We are never fully "healed," as there is always deeper and deeper and deeper to go until total enlightenment, but I've come such a long way, and so can you!

Always remember that everything is divinely timed and planned by the Universe. Trust it. It is always looking out for you, even when things don't feel that way. It all works out for everyone in the end, just as it's supposed to—even if it's not exactly how you would have chosen it to happen.

Nothing happens *to* us; it happens *for* us. Everything is always exactly as it's meant to be. Always.

LESSON THREE

What's Calling You Is Your Purpose

I was scared to go to college, but I couldn't imagine what else I would do instead. I certainly didn't want to stay stuck in our grief-filled house trying to console my dad and feeling the weight of my mom's loss, so off I went. I have a vague memory of riding around campus in a trolley with my father as part of orientation. It was beautiful, and I decided maybe things would be okay after all. I liked the idea of starting over where no one knew me.

I was really sad when Dad left (we were close now), so I got busy making my side of the room pretty. I hung up the flowery pictures and prints of abstract art I'd gotten along with my comforter at Bed, Bath & Beyond. I wanted that classic college experience and to live in the normal world—meaning, not one filled with crippling depression and grief—again.

But what's normal anyway? My roommate was Miss Teen Montana. Seriously. Sharing a tiny little room was new for us, but she was nice and cute. A few weeks into school, she got what seemed like a small cold, but then it kept getting worse. She went to the infirmary and never came back. I had no idea what had happened to her. Then the hall advisor announced she had gotten meningitis.

My next roommate was a nice, super academic who never slept because she was running for president of the school. She did nothing else but work and politics. She probably thought I was a hippie weirdo—I studied hard but nothing like the lengths she pushed herself to. I had trouble sleeping because she was up all hours studying, so let's just say we weren't an ideal match.

Eventually, I met a sweet girl who had a similar living style and moved in with her. She was always so easy to be around and gave me all the space I needed. We recently reconnected, and I was happy to find we still have a lot in common.

Even though I was going to class, making friends, smoking some pot, eating lots of calzones, and doing normal freshman stuff, I still couldn't help feeling different from everyone else. That negative thought had set into my mind when my mom was sick and only solidified when she died. Everyone else was partying around the clock and acting like, *Oh college, this is so much fun!* but that just wasn't my experience. Whether it was because I was still grieving, my introversion, or both, I spent a lot of time alone in my room even though I had some really cool friends.

One of those friends had lost her father, and so had this cute basketball player I had a crush on, so I decided to start a support group for kids who had lost a parent. I made a pitch to the psychology department, they accepted my proposal, and we started meeting on a regular basis. I didn't know it then, but I was being called to fulfill my purpose.

The group was mildly interesting and helpful—until I found out my crush on the soccer guy wasn't reciprocated. I could literally feel his pain, and it made me believe we had a huge connection that did not exist in reality. I stopped going to the group, and it fell apart pretty quickly after.

That year, I met my future (and now ex-) husband while I was crutching down the halls of my dorm. I was born with an extra bone in my ankle, so I'd just had it removed when I was home on break. He was on crutches, too, because of knee surgery from an old sports injury. I challenged him to a race, he won, and a great friendship started.

Meanwhile, I was dating a guy who was hot, smart, fun, and creative. Too bad he also periodically came completely unhinged. That was very attractive to me! Once I was ignoring him because we'd gotten into a fight, and he jumped on top of a table and wouldn't stop screaming my name when I walked into the cafeteria. That was his way to get my attention! Everyone was staring, and I practically died of embarrassment, but I still found him and his behavior attractive after that. Maybe even more so. I tended to like a little instability in men because it took me away from what I thought was the "boring" conventional world, which wasn't for me.

Eventually, he broke up with me, and I was heartbroken. He kept saying he wasn't good enough for me, and although I can see now that it wasn't healthy for me, at the time, I was devastated. Then he moved in with friends whom I'd introduced him to and started dating one of them, and it made me even sadder. I lurked around after classes waiting to see whom he was with and where he was going next. It was really pathetic.

My future husband was a friend and there for me during the breakup, and it made me start seeing him in a different light.

One weekend, I invited him to go to New York with me because I wanted to see what might happen between us. He probably didn't know what I had in mind when he said yes.

The weather was positively freezing, so we barely left the apartment. The only time we ventured out was to get pizza and calzones from this awesome place around the corner. Other than that, we stayed in, hung out, and got to know each other in a different way.

At the time, I needed grounding and caretaking, and that's exactly what he offered me. He wasn't unhinged. Instead, he was safe, "normal," driven, and had an idea of where he wanted to go and what he wanted to do with his life. Beyond those admirable qualities, though, hid another connection: he had lost his mother when he was young as well. I knew he must feel the same kind of deep loneliness I did. Once I realized that, I was like, *This is meant to be.*

Even though he was seeing someone else at the time, I knew he liked me. As soon as we got back to school, he broke up with her. He didn't tell her why, but she knew we had gone away together and threatened me physically. I was worried, especially because there were buildings at school named after this girl's family because her grandparents had made very generous endowments.

By this time, I was a senior in college, and my dad had started dating again. I was fine that he was getting out there because I wanted him to be happy, not alone and lonely. But then he started seeing—and later married—a woman whose soul felt so dark and terrifying to me. It was like I could see through her, and there was no love or authenticity to her. Of course now I'm able to see how traumatized she must have been. Her rageful vibe terrified me, and I automatically despised her.

I didn't realize it at the time, but I was totally reading her. I was—and still am, though I now know how to protect myself—an empathic sponge, so I picked up on all of her toxic energy. I realize now she was severely traumatized, fear-based, and lacking in any sort of self-love. Although I haven't been in contact with her for over thirteen years now, I hope she has healed since then.

As an empath, I always caught the wrath of her instability. She would make nasty comments and explode with anger. Once, when I was recovering from surgery, she started screaming at me about trouble she was having with her brother. I just sat there thinking, *Why is she screaming at me when this is about him?* I was young and scared of her emotional instability. My trauma kept piling up at this point.

It felt like she was trying to compete with me for my dad's love and attention. She would often complain about me to him; I felt so uncomfortable with this. I think my dad was able to see it after, but back then, he would get mad at me instead of calling her on her shit. I believe we all have a core purpose, and my dad's is to be a caretaker, so I guess it's not surprising he went from taking care of someone who was physically ill to someone with deep emotional issues. We all have so many lessons to learn!

The more I pushed her away, the more she tried to come after me. She was so jealous of me that it almost seemed like an obsession. She was always saying, "Oh my God, I didn't even lose my mom and I didn't know how to make friends at college. Look at how well you adjusted. How do you do it?" When I look back now through different eyes, I have compassion for her and how "lacking of love" she was. Now I see that all behavior like this is just a "call for love." But of course, back then, I had no clue of this.

At my college graduation, my friend Terra had a party at her house. I had always been envious of Terra because she had the nicest parents and a normal family. She had started to work as a teenager to cover her expenses, and she never seemed to feel empty or sad. I always had money from my dad, but it never made me feel better, so I thought maybe if I'd been made to work, I wouldn't feel empty or sad either. Who knows? Terra made me wish I'd had better guidance and been encouraged to occupy myself more. Money is definitely not the answer to everything like many people believe. Love is.

As usual, my stepmother ruined the party for me (as well as many after that). She blew a fit and told my dad I wasn't being inclusive or nice to her. It made me want to leave early because I was in such a bad mood (not knowing I was absorbing her miserable energy). Like a child, everything was always about her. I literally hadn't done or said anything wrong, but he got mad at me anyway. I was like, *I'm twenty-one, and even I know she needs to grow up and heal.* But like a true empath (I didn't know I was at the time), I was left feeling bad and guilty for her issues.

Now, as a mom, I see why healing is so important and how amazing millennials and Gen Z and the generations to follow are. These are the first generations (and some from others as well) to begin to really heal themselves to not continue "generational trauma" to be passed on. I'm grateful that I've woken up to this for myself to be able to teach my kids from a balanced place (I'm still learning) where my inner child is healing and not vomiting up my issues of everyone I come in contact with. (I used to do this and have no awareness of it.)

But unfortunately, my dad being in that relationship changed *our* relationship. Even though he may still have been physically present, he became emotionally absent during that time. I see now how this was his "escape" from the pain. I'd already lost my mom; this made it like I was losing my dad, too. My sister was starting to be absent as well now. I didn't feel I had a "family" like everyone else did. Years later, after my dad and stepmother divorced, my aunt said to me, "You're so lucky he chose you. A lot of men don't do that." I was like, *Wow, that's really great.*

When I graduated, with no mother, a distant father, a difficult stepmother, an absent sister (once she went away to college, she disconnected herself from our family), and a piece of paper that said I had a degree in psychology, I had no idea what to do next. I couldn't move back to my dad's house with my stepmother there. I felt like I had nowhere to be, nowhere to go, and no one who wanted me.

When a friend suggested joining her on a trip to South America, I jumped at the chance. I just wanted a break, but what I got was something else altogether—another giant trauma, to be exact. Remember, we all signed up for the lessons we learn in life, but that doesn't make it any easier or more fun when we're going through them.

My friend and I were having a great time in Ecuador until one night when we were walking back to our hostel after dinner. Three guys jumped us, held a piece of glass to my friend's neck, and demanded our bags and money. They took everything and left us there, shaking and terrified. I can still picture it like it was yesterday, even though it feels like a lifetime and another person ago. I now know when we are in a low place or "low vibration" we attract low-vibing experiences into our lives. That's what was happening for me now. Think about yourself and your own life, and you will see the correlation. Now I'm on such a higher vibe. The experiences and people I attract are so loving and beautiful. It's amazing. The law of attraction: We attract what we are.

They say humans have three responses to danger: fight, flight, or freeze. I guess my go-to is freeze. I felt so bad that I didn't do anything to help when the thief was threatening my friend, but I literally couldn't move or even look away. It was like I was stuck to the ground. I had guilt about that for years, but honestly, what could I have done? Grabbed for the glass and gotten killed? That wouldn't have helped anyone.

We were physically okay but definitely traumatized. When we went to the cops, they did nothing. They were corrupt, laughing, and in on it with the thieves. They flirted with us and didn't seem to care at all. Luckily, some "earth angels" greeted us back at the hostel—men and women who were so nurturing, nice, and supportive to us. They helped us feel safe and secure again.

Since then, I've learned there are *always* angels to be found. No matter how bad the situation seems, they're there—we just have to look for them. For example, while I lost my mother early, later on in my life at various jobs I had, a woman around the same age my mom would have been always appeared as a new friend when I needed her most. I appreciate her gifting me these earth angels to help support me on my journey.

When I got home from that trip, my future husband told me he was moving to LA for a job. I thought to myself, *LA sounds fun and it has beautiful weather. It's as far away from New York as possible and as far away from my problems as I can get in this country. Why not go there, too?* I liked him, and we were close, but my decision was more about running away and escaping than anything else. I was like, *Can I come?* and he said sure.

Once I got to California, I worked a bunch of different jobs. I bartended at private parties and was hired at a group home, counseling children who had been removed from their families. I sold tickets on the Santa Monica Pier to be in the studio audience of the *Rosie O'Donnell Show*. I had no direction and was not grounded. I was just flying by the seat of my pants.

I stayed in LA for only eleven months. Although I had been ignoring my purpose, the plan in my brain had always been to go back to school to become a psychotherapist. The choice was between NYU and Pepperdine, and I picked NYU and NYC in the end.

Something was calling me back east. My dad, childhood friends, aunt, and cousins were all there. It felt like the Universe was guiding me toward something familiar and stable.

I was going home—whatever that was at this point.

WHAT I NOW KNOW

Whatever you're drawn to and lights you up is what you're meant to do and will often turn out to be your purpose and passion. So if you feel called to do something and it brings you joy, then by all means, go and do it. Follow your bliss and you will find your purpose. I was drawn to study psychology in school, helping those kids in LA who had been taken from their parents, and then grad school to become a psychotherapist because I wanted to help ease people's pain in the same way I was trying to ease mine, but your purpose and passion doesn't have to be job related. It could be gardening or volunteering or yoga or raising kids or writing poetry. It might be something so simple you don't even think it's worth pursuing, but it always is. When you light up, you will help pave the way for others to light up as well.

Concentrate your time on the things you do well. Develop your gifts. Create a life that brings you peace and joy.

The Universe runs very nicely when we all focus on what we're really good at and are excited about doing. Let other people handle the things you're not interested in or skilled at. It's like me with technology. My friends and kids are always laughing at me saying, *It's so easy. Let me show you*, but I continue to have so much difficulty. I'm like, *No, I talk to dead people and do spiritual healing. That's my gift. You do you, and I'll do me!*

Focus on what feels good and natural and lights you up inside. If you don't know what that is, it's time to explore different hobbies, interests, and professions to find out. Go where the light and joy is! It's there.

We were all given special gifts for a reason. That is our passion and purpose. Light up the world with your gifts, and let that guide the way for others to do so as well.

Follow the Universe, the flow, and whatever lights up your soul. Listen to your inner guidance and nothing else. No one knows what's best for you but you. It's fine to consult others for support and guidance, but in the end, only you know what you need. Trust that. Don't waste time living a life that doesn't feel peaceful to you. Live authentically and be vulnerable. It's so worth it.

What calls to you is what you're meant to pursue—professionally and personally.

LESSON FOUR

Helping Others Helps *You*

Back in New York, some parts of my life got better, and others remained very challenging.

The positive: I got a studio apartment in the same building as my best friend from childhood, and other high school friends were nearby. (We were very *Sex in the City* during the time while the show was hot.) My dad was still working in Manhattan, so every week, we went out for dinner. We'd meet at an Italian restaurant called Bistango, the Hudson Grill, or Lanaam (our favorite Asian noodle place) and catch up while we ate everything in sight. On the way out, he'd always give a homeless person his leftovers, a generous amount of money, and a strong guidance to clean up their life. My dad is a good man, always was. Like everyone, he does the best he can from where he's at consciously; that's all we can do. He didn't have an easy life at all, came from nothing and did well for himself. I was proud he was my dad. I felt more connected than I had in a long time, and that's what I needed—human connection.

The difficult: I still felt weird and different. Lonely. I was unconsciously picking up on the energy of the millions of people who lived in the city, and there's no worse place to be than New York City—the concrete jungle—to be ungrounded like that. Looking back now, I can see that my psychic and empathic abilities were out of control, and I had no boundaries. I truly didn't know where I ended and other people began. I was floating around.

By the time I started classes for graduate school at NYU, I was feeling so shy, awkward, and invisible that I was afraid to talk. I just couldn't find my voice. My throat chakra, which is all about standing up for yourself and speaking your truth, was still completely blocked as it had been since my teens. (After that, I'd gone in the other direction and my throat chakra was wide open. Now I'm more balanced, somewhere in the middle, and that is best.)

There was a girl from my high school in the program, too. She seemed so perfect and was always answering questions in class and seemed to enjoy it. I was like, *Oh my God, she probably thinks*

I'm so strange. She was just so present while I was like a disassociated ungrounded chicken with my head cut off.

I knew I had to figure out how to dig myself out of the dark hole I'd been in since before my mom died, so I found a therapist and started going to see her. I liked her even though she didn't seem very confident in herself either—she was sweet but always giggled nervously, which was weird when we were talking about serious things. What a great pair we were! Still, I felt safe with her, and it was a start down the right path.

Now this: It was early in the morning before my first class, during my first few weeks of grad school. I was in my new giggly therapist's office; it was a small and cute office right by NYU. All of a sudden, we heard screaming outside. We scrambled over to the window—the noise was *that* unexpected and disturbing—only to see tons of people running up the street. A lot of them were crying. Everyone was heading north.

WTF?

We had no idea what was going on. To be fair, no one knew yet that those planes had flown into the Twin Towers on purpose and our country had just been attacked. What we did know was that there was smoke everywhere, and we needed to get away from it like everyone else. We were close to Ground Zero.

The minute we got downstairs, my therapist got swallowed up in the crowd, and I was left in a sea of screaming, crying strangers. It was so overwhelming. I could feel everyone's terror like it was my own. And the smell! It was awful. I could taste the burning chemicals in my mouth. Even now, more than twenty years later, I can still taste it.

I looked up and watched the second plane hit tower two. My brain couldn't comprehend what I was seeing. It felt like I was watching a horror movie unfolding before my eyes. I just kept running. It was all so surreal.

As I ran, I was gripped with terror that my dad had been killed in the attack. His office wasn't in the World Trade Center anymore, but my brain went into panic mode because he'd been in the bombing of 1993 there. Back then, my mom was still alive, and we'd waited for news about my dad at a family friend's house. It was so traumatizing not knowing if he was okay for much of that long day, but at least we'd been together. I was alone now and was freaking out at the thought of being left parentless.

I kept trying to reach my dad but couldn't get through, so I started calling everyone I knew in New York. Finally, I got in touch with an old friend I hadn't seen in a while who was living with people from her college. With nowhere else to go, I headed to her place, even though we weren't close anymore. I felt so lost, alone, and out of place even after I got there.

Eventually, I found out my dad was safe and had been working at his Midtown office at the time of the bombing. My relief at finding out he was alive was followed quickly by disappointment. A lot of my friends had already gone safely to their parents' house to stay, but he didn't ask me if I wanted to come home—he just headed to Long Island to be with my stepmom. She definitely didn't tell him to invite me. After what I'd just witnessed, I had a strong desire to be taken care of, but that was not in the cards. I felt more alone. That was a "theme" in my life.

After 9/11, New York City felt like the Twilight Zone and looked apocalyptic. I will never forget the utter destruction, devastation, and loss in the air, but New Yorkers are so strong and resilient. Everyone was holding each other up during that time. My future husband flew in from LA (we were in a long-distance relationship then, meeting each other in the middle of the country), and we went to see Ground Zero together.

About a week later, I was walking down the street when I saw a big crowd of people in the street. The cops were there, too. I stopped and looked up. A woman was on a ledge, ready to jump off the roof of a building. Everyone was just staring, paralyzed by the scene that was unfolding. I called the friend I was on my way to meet on my flip phone (they were very in at the time), and she told me to put my head down and walk away. *Whatever you do, don't look*, she said. Once again, I froze. I was so scared that I couldn't move a muscle.

The woman dropped onto the sidewalk right in front of me, and I immediately threw up and fell to the ground. I'll never forget that vision in my head, even now so many years later. As I write this, I can feel the lovely energy of the woman I saw take her own life over twenty years ago. I later found out her husband died the week earlier on 9/11 and she went to be with him.

A kind stranger (an older woman) took care of me even though she was surely traumatized as well. She helped me stand up and call my friend—another earth angel sent by my mom. At the time, I felt horrified and powerless, but now that I know how to use my abilities, I always project healing love to everyone when I find myself in these types of situations. I notice now that the Universe always puts me in close proximity to car accidents or other traumatic events happening so I am able to send healing energy to the victims.

This is a thing with spiritual connectors and healers—we tend to work with specific groups because those souls are drawn to us.

Suicides, overdoses, and young kids always seem to come to me. I'm told by the dead that because I've felt suicidal myself, they feel safe with me. I never judge them and nothing shocks me, which is probably also why I spent my early years as a psychotherapist being a substance abuse counselor. As for the kids, I love children so much and their energy is the best. Often, I act just like them.

As you might imagine, after witnessing 9/11 and a suicide within the span of a week (piling up with my other past traumas), I was anxious, depressed, and couldn't see the point in much of anything. People were walking around NYC holding signs and looking for their loved ones, but I felt dead people all around me, so I knew they were searching in vain. That horrific smell hung over the city, a toxic cocktail of charred flesh and steel, poisonous gases, misery, pain, and fear. I'm not a fan of all the mask-wearing now, but we should have had them back then. We were breathing that gross stuff all day.

By this point, I'm sure I was running on adrenaline and cortisol for many years—stress hormones that can really damage our health in the long term—but I didn't know how to get myself out of that evolutionary fight-or-flight response. I can see now how all these traumas contributed to my extreme anxiety and the eventual deterioration of my adrenal glands. I've since healed them with the help of different holistic treatments (acupuncture, meditation, vitamins, etc.) after years of trauma and depletion.

Today, I treat my body like a temple. Healing and nurturing it in every way is the most important thing to me. Our bodies are our homes, and I'm so grateful for my beautiful, healthy body and all it does for me. Back then, though, I was a mess. A walking panic attack.

I went back to school and somehow intuitively figured out connecting with nature helped me calm down. This wasn't always so easy to find in NYC. Whenever I started to freak out, I'd sprint to whatever grassy place was closest. Sitting on a bench and just breathing in the air at Madison Square Park was my favorite. Other times, I'd make it up to Central Park and get lost in an area where there were no humans. There were so many people everywhere I looked in NYC. NYC isn't exactly the place to go to relax and heal from trauma. When it wasn't winter, I'd always take my shoes off and put my feet directly on the earth, not knowing back then that the name for what I was doing was grounding, or earthing, myself. I also took a lot of showers and a nightly bath because they brought me some measure of comfort. Without knowing it, I was clearing my body of the day's energies. As a healer, I now teach people to go barefoot or hug a tree to reconnect with the earth and get immersed in water to cleanse themselves of negative vibes. My body intuitively did this. Our bodies are very smart and know what we need. Our loud minds just get in the way.

As part of my grad program, we were placed in internships to get experience doing counseling and therapy. My first one was with sexually abused and neglected children. Most of them had drug-addicted or alcoholic parents. One cutie I worked with had eaten lead paint. I connected with their loneliness, their loss—we all had being motherless or parentless in common. If you've experienced nothing and had an extremely blessed life, you're not going to be drawn into this field. Like I said before, I was the "wounded healer."

My next internship was at an NYC psychiatric hospital, in the mentally ill/chemically abusing unit. As a young woman, I found the place quite scary as well as abusive in many ways. My supervisor and some other staff members were so angry and miserable. I now see how hard it was to do the work that they did every day.

Inside, the atmosphere wasn't welcoming. Illegal drugs ran rampant on the floor. Even though I knew it wasn't their fault because they came from terrible circumstances and never had a chance, I found many of the male patients there threatening and inappropriate. Once, I was counseling a man when he started getting totally agitated. We were alone in the room and he had a violent history, so I went to get help. Thankfully, two male social workers there were protective of me in a very paternal way (angels again). They made sure I never had to be alone with that guy again.

Another student told me my advisor would pull me out of there if I requested it—apparently, a lot of other interns were doing that—but even though I wanted to leave, I thought I should stick it out and be strong. Asking to leave seemed entitled to me, like I couldn't hack it. I now completely disagree with that way of thinking and know to follow my intuition and only go where I feel good and peaceful. Being in my peace only contributes to the peace of the world. Back then, even though I cried in the bathroom every morning, I decided, *They assigned me to this for a reason, and I'm not going to quit.* I was so freaking happy when that placement was over. I felt I'd beyond paid my dues! Looking back now, I can see all that I learned from that placement.

After I finished NYU grad school, I started working full time at Green House with people experiencing substance abuse issues. Whereas NYC Square was a public hospital and pretty much all of the patients were from terrible circumstances, Green House had a more diverse population. The people there might be famous, wealthy, or really successful on Wall Street or they might be homeless. It was a wide range, and I never knew who would be admitted next. Addiction doesn't discriminate.

Some of my clients were even the same age as me, which seemed so weird at the time. I remember working with one young guy who was struggling with alcohol, cocaine, and sex addictions. He was very smart and so cute. He worked in finance but was always getting fired over doing drugs and fucking people he wasn't supposed to. We had such a nice connection, and I feel like I helped him a lot. Many years later, I saw him on Instagram and it looked like he was doing well. It seems he's finally sober now, but it took a long time for him to get his life on track.

Another patient I loved working with was a guy named Esteban. He was in his fifties, a heroin addict with HIV and cognitive issues. He was obsessed with me, not in a scary way but a cute, tender, friendly way. I once ran into him at a park with a friend and he was over-the-top excited to see me. It was so sweet. He thought I was amazing, smart, beautiful, talented, and had it all together, which was great after feeling invisible for so long.

Esteban relapsed a lot, and even though he never fully got better, I knew that was part of it—some people aren't meant to recover. Their contract with the Universe isn't written that way. Years later, after discovering my gifts as a medium, I am able to feel when people whom I've lost touch with have passed over. They come and say hello to me. It is beautiful and bittersweet. Esteban has done that.

Another patient I'll never forget had gone to jail for way too many years for selling pot. I liked and admired her. She was very smart and high functioning and was doing a lot of good work to reform drug laws while she was getting her master's degree. MSNBC came to do a piece on her, and I was so excited when my colleague and good friend Karen and I were chosen to be in it.

There was also another gorgeous young guy named Derrick who was a patient of mine. He was an alcoholic and a sex addict. He slept with many celebrities in NYC but was so lonely and empty inside. He was in so much pain that I could identify with. I had a huge crush on him but tried to keep it very professional. Over fifteen years later, I'm happy to see him recently on Instagram sober with a great job and family. I wonder about so many past clients, so seeing something like this makes me happy. Everyone has their own story.

The work at Green House was always fascinating, and my tenure there was extremely beneficial to me. I discovered I was good at the work I was doing. I loved connecting to and helping others.

The patients there were exciting—from different backgrounds, with different problems, and different degrees of willingness to heal. No matter their circumstances, I always saw the good in them. On the inside, we're all the same, right? We all want to be loved and at peace.

As a bonus, I made a close group of friends on the job. My coworkers and I were all in our twenties and early thirties, and we had a blast together despite the intense atmosphere. After every session with a patient, we'd come back and discuss what happened and how to be more effective in the future. We'd all go out to lunch—especially to this Cuban place right next door—and happy hours together. It really felt like a family.

Karen and I were so close that we became like sisters. Our supervisor, David, was a sweet, gentle father figure. Another coworker, Deb, treated me with such a loving maternal energy that I called her my work mom. Tom and Amir were like the brothers I never had, so nice and safe. Veronica the intern became one of my closest friends. I can see how it was all so very healing for me. Years later, I've since lost touch with them, but that place and those people will always hold a hugely special place in my heart.

For the first time in a very long time, I felt supported. Loved. Seen. Successful. The darkness began to lift as I discovered my passion, purpose, and place in the world.

WHAT I NOW KNOW

Giving and helping others actually helps *you*. Sometimes you just need to take the attention off yourself and put your energies into someone or something else. Things start looking up when you're learning, interacting, and connecting with other humans and their stories. Of course, do not "take from you" to give to others. Always "fill your cup" up first or "put your seat belt" on first or you will be depleted and have nothing for you and others.

When faced with a problem, most people either want to fix it or give advice. They'll say, *Oh, that happened to me; here's how I handled it.* If that sounds like something you tend to do, try to simply witness the other person's emotions next time. Holding space (my favorite phrase) like that shows you accept that person and everything they're going through. You're not trying to change anything, but you're able to sit in their feelings with them and "hold that space" for them.

Fixing the problem would be defeating the purpose anyway. They're not asking you to fix it. That's our own anxiety with wanting to make the uncomfortable feelings go away. Just acknowledge what they're saying and feeling. Validate them in the way you wish you were validated. That might be hard, but it tells the person, *I'm here with you. I'm with you in this.* That's an incredible gift in and of itself.

Sometimes, having someone lovingly sit with us through our pain is all we all need to feel seen and better. When someone does that—like I did for my patients then and do for my clients now—it can be the most healing thing in the world. It can be very heavy to sit with the pain of another, so make sure you're taking care of yourself.

Balance is always key. Self-love, self-care, and boundaries are so very important to your well-being. Follow your heart and intuition when you need to take space from humans as well. Check in to see how you are feeling throughout the day and see what it is that you need. Your needs are so very important. You come first.

Helping others also offers a great perspective on life. We're all so immersed in our own shit, and we all think our situation is the worst, but that's just not true. Things could always be worse. As Wayne Dyer, one of the most famous spiritual teachers in the world (and my all-time fave), once said, "When you change the way you look at things, the things you look at change." This is so very true.

I've been guided by his words, teachings, and spirit along my path to becoming a spiritual healer. I even felt him sitting next to me at lunch a few years ago. The friend I was with, one of my besties—Nora—who is also very spiritual and has her own abilities, said, "Erica, Wayne Dyer is sitting next to you." I didn't even bring it up; she just saw him! Amazing. Then to further confirm this, the Universe somehow connected me with one of his loved ones for a session and he came through loud and clear. He works through me often now and wants his messages to stay alive in this world while he's in the spirit world. I'm honored to learn from him and share his teachings. That's how the magical Universe works.

Anything that takes the spotlight off your problems and focuses attention on someone else is the thing to do when you need some perspective and you are guided by the Universe to do so. There's so much magic in being of service. There's so much more out there for you.

So go do something! Get out of your routine and bubble. Volunteer. Connect with something that's calling you. Tell someone they're beautiful. Connect with a stranger, Listen to a friend who is having a tough time without reaching for solutions or advice.

Help someone else, and pretty soon you'll find out what you're *actually* doing is helping yourself.

LESSON FIVE

Grounding Is Everything

At the same time I transitioned to full-time work at Greenwich House as a substance abuse therapist, I started going for a post-master's certification in psychodynamic psychotherapy at NYU. It was going to take two more years of school at night, but I loved it and was determined to become a therapist and start my own practice.

Future husband was still living in LA. We'd spent the last two years meeting in the middle of the country—Chicago, St. Louis, wherever, whenever—and I was over the long-distance thing. We had a good thing going, so why not keep it going in the same city?

He quickly landed a job as a reporter at a gossip magazine in NYC. So now future husband and I were living together in New York. I had a job I loved. I was continuing my education, and it seemed like the pieces of my life were all falling into place.

I started seeing a new therapist, Maggie, to work on all that, as well as the trauma that was still brewing in me. I connected with her to the point where she felt like another earth angel. She was very maternal, strong, and similar to my mom. Just a great, grounded human. I loved Maggie.

I also loved sitting in her office. It was ornate to the point of almost being gaudy—there were so many expensive decorations—yet at the same time, it was messy and scattered. Papers were piled everywhere. This made her seem very real to me.

She saved me more than once during our time together. She was maternal and stable and "alive" and present and showed me different ways of looking at situations. She helped to calm me down and "ground" me when my emotions were spiraling "out of control" and gave me some direction as I was so scattered in my life. She always pointed out that I don't need to tell everyone everything that was going on in my life (to seek external validation) and I can be more discerning. This has taken me years to fully grasp, but finally I get how important and sacred my life and my energy is. So many years later, I always want to visit her when I visit NYC, but I haven't done it yet. She's probably in her eighties and retired now.

Once future husband and I had been dating for five years, I was like, *Come on, what are we doing here?* We had talked about getting engaged, so when we went to a nice hotel out on Greenpoint, Long Island, for the weekend, I was pretty much expecting the proposal. We were taking a walk in these beautiful green fields when he asked me to marry him.

Of course I said yes. I was so happy we were going to be making a life together.

Our wedding day didn't exactly turn out to be as magical as people make that stuff out to be, though. Every girl needs her mom there, and that was very hard for me. In Jewish weddings, both parents walk you down the aisle, and my stepmom insisted on being included even though that wasn't at all what I wanted. My dad told me, *You have to let her walk you down the aisle.* I was like, *I don't like her. She's not my mother and she's not nice to me.* But he was always trying to put out fires and she was so difficult, so I eventually gave in.

Although I'd asked my sister to be in my wedding party with my friends, I was also concerned about what her emotional state was going to be on my wedding day. Having her little sister get married before her was rough for her, and she had some mental health issues she was dealing with. Once when I was in grad school, working at the psychiatric hospital, I got a call from her apartment building manager that her bathtub was leaking water into the apartment below hers. Of course my mind jumped to the worst conclusion. Thankfully, it turned out she was physically fine and not even home at the time, but her frequent disappearances and calls like that one added to my trauma and abandonment issues. At twenty-two years old, this was heavy stuff for me. I was doing better in many respects but still a mess in others.

My main concern at the moment, however, was whether she was going to be on time. (Yes.) Was she going to be emotional? (Yes, again.) I think she was happy for me, but sad for herself. I understand now she meant no harm to me and was just trying to process her own complicated emotions. Now, so many years later—we haven't seen each other in sixteen years—I respect her boundaries and choice to disconnect from our family. I had to grow up and do a ton of healing and spiritual work around this to see this. I used to take her absence personally, like I did something wrong, but I now know everyone has to do in life what's right for them. It's not our job to judge their journey. I will forever love her and hope to see her again in this lifetime. If not, I know we will meet again in the next one. Whatever is meant to be, will be, always. Doesn't mean it's less painful, just means it is exactly how it's supposed to be.

Another friend who was in my wedding party had similar emotional struggles as my sister with me getting married. She locked herself in the wedding closet and sobbed the whole time I was getting ready. She could not separate my happiness from her unhappiness. That was difficult for us both.

Due to my lack of groundedness and boundaries as an empath, I took on all this negative energy. Getting bombarded by other people's emotions was too much for me. I didn't realize I could speak up about how I was feeling. Honestly, I didn't even know how to. I hated everyone generating that crappy low vibe, and then I felt bad about hating them. It all sucked. Of course, back then I didn't know I had a choice in the matter—that I could set my own boundaries and ground myself. I do remember my cousin Kim and a couple of my other friends being such a bright light of support that day.

The person I am today would never allow that, but I have good boundaries and have carefully curated who is in my life so it wouldn't even be an issue today. The people I'm close to love and support me and bring me so much joy. They elevate and amplify my happiness. I'm forever grateful for these people.

Not that I regret my wedding day. All of our struggles make us stronger and make up our journey and story. I know what I want and who is allowed into my life. I decide all of that and have since manifested the peaceful and beyond magical life of my dreams.

Anyhow, I tried to make the best of what was going on behind the scenes and move on from the drama, and there were definitely some great moments. The reception was black tie and everyone looked so elegant. The party was held at a beautiful space overlooking the Hudson. The reception was decorated with sparkling candles and gorgeous white flowers. I did have fun with my friends and husband, dancing up a storm.

Right after, Husband and I headed to Hawaii for our honeymoon. Because I was still immersed in the energy and drama of our wedding day, I wasn't able to be fully happy and enjoy the moment. I've since learned there's nothing more important than being present. Getting stuck in the past causes depression, and ruminating on what might happen in the future causes anxiety. The present moment is truly all we have. As the saying goes, *Wherever you are, be there.*

After our honeymoon, I was over things only being about me and all the stuff I'd experienced. I was ready to give my energy to another human. People say you never really know when you're ready for kids, but I did. I was ready. The intuition I didn't know I had yet was telling me it was time to bring two angels into the world. Husband maybe wasn't as ready as me, but we decided to go for it.

Almost two years after our wedding, I sadly had a miscarriage and was devastated, but then shortly after, I got pregnant again. We were thrilled. I recently found myself at the Barnes & Noble in Union Square fifteen years after the birth of my first daughter and realized that was where I found out I was pregnant with her. I have no idea why I decided to take a pregnancy test at a giant bookstore in the middle of New York City, but being there brought back the memory of the utter bliss and excitement I felt in that moment. Today, I'm still blown away that I grew two miraculous humans inside of me.

The tiny studio we'd been living in wasn't going to be big enough for both of us and a baby, so we signed a lease for a two-bedroom apartment in the original building I'd been in when I first moved back to New York. We paid so much NYC rent, but the apartment was gross. It was infested with rats, and everything was falling apart. One day, the ceiling basically caved in. We already had a crib set up in the corner, and if baby C had been in there at the time, she would have been severely injured.

My pregnancy became difficult almost immediately. Even though I was young and in good shape, I developed severe gestational diabetes. Doctors had a hard time balancing my blood sugar. I needed multiple insulin shots throughout the day.

It got so I was always at the doctor's office. My life turned into an endless cycle of making sure the baby was okay. My entire day was consumed by giving myself shots, testing my blood, meeting with nutritionists, and seeing doctors. Eventually, it got so overwhelming and time-consuming that I had to quit work. I believe if I'd had the benefit of the health knowledge I've acquired since then, it would have been a very different experience.

My mom missing out on my pregnancy and children's births was extremely difficult for me. When I look back now, I wonder if I in essence willed myself sick so medical professionals would give me some kind of motherly care as she would have in that situation. As humans, we seek out what we need and get our needs met somehow, whether that's in a healthy or unhealthy way. We manifest everything in our lives for the lessons we need to learn. This happens everywhere, all the time, but we can only see it in retrospect. It was unconscious to me then, but looking back, it is so clear to me now. I needed to be taken care of by someone, so I was. The medical professionals I saw back then were just more angels my mom put into my life.

The Universe must have known how desperate I was to have family and connection because when I was at the doctor's office, my cousin happened to be there, too. At the time, it seemed like such a crazy coincidence, but I now know there are no coincidences, only synchronicities of the Universe. We were both motherless and pregnant, and our mothers who had already passed brought us together to support each other.

My cousin's mom—my dad's sister—had died about seven years earlier. I was just starting to get to know her when she got sick with breast cancer. While she was in the hospital, I felt called to go see her. I now know it was because she wanted to connect me and my cousin before she passed. The Universe always sets everything up so perfectly.

When I showed up in my aunt's hospital room that day, it was scary. She was really sick. She started talking to me about my husband, wishing me luck with him. It was a bittersweet visit because the minute I left the room, a nurse came out and announced she had just died.

Afterward, I was hugging my cousin in the hallway when we both distinctly heard her mom call out her name. No one else was around, but it was clear as day. My cousin wasn't so into this psychic stuff, but even she couldn't deny what we'd heard. I am so grateful I was there to support her and witness her mom's final goodbye. I guess that was also a sign so many years before I knew I was a medium of my abilities to communicate with the dead. My cousin has had some of these experiences, too, but like so many other people chose to "block" them out.

We chalked it up to a random crazy thing, but once again, nothing is random and there are no coincidences. Everything is magically created by the divine Universe to help us to learn and evolve. That was my first mediumship experience even though I didn't know it at the time.

Now back to the day I gave birth to baby C. The rest of the day that we saw each other at the doctor's office was like a movie scene. I wasn't dilated at all, but the doctor broke my water to get labor going anyway. I was in so much pain, but I guess that's just what they do in New York City to get the babies out quickly! My labor began and we hailed a cab, anxious and in a hurry to meet my impending arrival. It was like a movie scene as my mother-in-law at the time and I rushed to the hospital. My cousin, my dad, my husband, and his father arrived later, along with my aunt Gail.

Of course, then it took a full twenty-four hours until baby C was born. Nature can't be rushed, even in NYC. Tired and high from the epidural, I was absolutely thrilled when baby C was born healthy. She was the cutest, tiniest little angel.

I was also happy to be taken care of in a hospital, although I was in the male urology unit because of overcrowding during Christmastime. I had an older male neighbor, and there was only a curtain between us. It was not the best situation to welcome a new baby into. I made sure it didn't happen again during my next labor with my second delicious mushball.

I was ecstatic to be a new mom and felt really confident when the nurses were helping me care for my baby in the hospital. When we got home, though, it was a totally different story. I started worrying about the typical stuff, but I had no one to help me navigate my new role. I was so fearful, and my hormones were completely out of whack.

Everything became overwhelming after that, especially since Husband went right back to work on his same busy schedule. I didn't have a tribe of new moms to rely on yet. It was difficult and lonely for me to manage a newborn's needs without the support or guidance of my own mom.

My life had been turned upside down, but everyone else was busy with their regular lives, especially my friends. None of them were married yet, let alone had kids. They were all still out partying and looking for guys. I felt disconnected from them, like I was on an island all my own. I was ungrounded and scattered.

Before long, I started to feel like I was losing my mind. I wasn't sleeping. I couldn't sit still. I was crying a lot. I even started having panic attacks. My post-pregnancy hormones were out of control.

One day I told my husband, "I just need to relax." He told me to calm down, and he took baby C. My amazing friend Veronica came to help him out with her, and I went to my dad's house in Long Island. He tried to assure me I was fine, but it felt like I was literally outside my body. I made him take me to the hospital, where I was diagnosed with postpartum anxiety and depression.

Postpartum anxiety can feel a lot like psychosis, but all I needed was the tiniest little sliver of Ativan to feel better. What a relief that was. A psychiatrist also prescribed a small dose of Lexapro to help with my anxiety, and that was all I needed to regain my footing in the world.

After a rough start, Husband and I fell in love with our new lifestyle as young parents. We got into a good routine, and motherhood became a great role for me. I went back to work part time and started seeing a few private clients.

Throughout it all, I adored my delicious little, smiling, giggling mushball. She was so angelic and beautiful, a happy angel. Babies and kids are my favorite, so light and free, no societal conditioning yet. They are also very connected to the spiritual world, having recently come from there.

We then quickly decided to have another baby. Make that, I decided I wanted another baby. I started thinking it would be great for Chloe to have a buddy and was like, *Let's go!* Once again, Husband wasn't quite as ready as I was, but eventually he got there. I tend to move very quickly when I know what I want; this is hard sometimes for others who take things a little slower.

Fortunately, I got pregnant quickly. Unfortunately, the gestational diabetes was even worse this time. I was at the doctor three times a week so they could monitor my cutie-pie's health, and I was checking my blood and taking many insulin shots a day. I had to stop working again.

At thirty-seven weeks, the doctors tested my new baby girl's lungs. Once they were convinced she would be able to breathe on her own, they took baby L out. Because I was still on Lexapro, I didn't have to deal with postpartum anxiety. What a relief! Of course having two little ones, combined with the frantic big-city energy, was still overwhelming.

After feeling so alone, I now had the love and adoration of two beautiful baby girls who relied on me. They were so in love with each other, which was amazingly cute to watch. Silly besties from day one. I was finally in a good place with my life. I was feeling happier. The next few years were a blur of sleepless nights and nonstop kiddie birthday parties and meeting some "mommy" friends and couples.

Next in NYC, we began to interview for kindergarten, which seemed insane to me. Husband was really into it and wanted to make sure Chloe was going to receive the best education. I agreed in theory, but the entire process made me feel nervous, anxious, overwhelmed, like I was headed right back to where I started, which wasn't a place I wanted to revisit. And for what? This nonstop, crazy, competitive way of life didn't feel like the way to happiness or peace to me.

I knew there had to be a better way for us to be grounded and happy. A better way for us to raise kids. A better life for us waiting for us somewhere else. I just didn't know exactly where yet or how fast it would happen for us.

WHAT I NOW KNOW

I was so scattered and ungrounded during my young adulthood. Along with my throat chakra, my root chakra, which is our grounding and connection to the earth, was blocked. And even though my upper chakras—the third eye and the crown, which are all about psychic energy—were flowing, they were a bit too open. I didn't know what to do with the information I was picking up all the time. As a result, I was never present and very unbalanced.

When the root chakra is flowing and connected, we feel grounded and stable. When the upper chakras are open, we are totally tuned into the psychic energy surrounding us. But when the upper chakras are too open and the root chakra is closed, we start to feel unbalanced and even "outside of our body." I know this sounds confusing. I invite you to read about this if it sounds interesting to you. We are energetic beings and our chakras are our specific energy centers. Unbalanced and "out of my body" is exactly what had happened to me. Now I work hard at balancing my chakras and help others do the same.

During stressful times, people tend to feel scattered because they're not grounded in their body, thus living *outside* of their bodies. When someone is really grounded, they're connected to their own body—they're not all over the place. Even if they're psychic, they're not taking on stuff that belongs to other people. That's why meditation and other "grounding" activities are so important all of the time, and especially during times of stress.

I was so out of whack, but I was eventually able to heal my adrenals and my nervous system with the help of my mentor Nicola at the time and through meditation, nutrition, exercise, yoga, self-love, only being around good nurturing people, nature, and other self-care practices. I didn't realize that I, as many of you are, was living in fight or flight for twenty years, but I am now balanced and regulated and medication-free from doing intensive healing work.

A great way to balance, regulate, and ground yourself is through meditation. If you don't like the word "meditation," substitute the word "breath" for it. Our breath is our source of everything. It's our source of life. Our source of *spirit*. It's all simply a matter of slowing everything down, taking deep breaths, and going within.

My advice whenever you're feeling ungrounded or like you're spiraling is to take a step back, sit, and just breathe. If you don't want to sit, head outdoors. Swim in the ocean or a pool. Walk barefoot and touch sand or dirt. Nothing grounds you more than nature and meditation. If you can't do any of this, look at pictures of nature and listen to relaxing music. Have a quiet moment, and be in peace and stillness. It's also so important to "feel" all your feelings and allow them to flow and be present, then try to let them go at your own pace when you're ready. Express gratitude for all the abundance that you have, do not focus on the lack of what you don't have. I see now that I always had the choice to focus on all the abundance in my life instead of the lack I experienced. Abundance is love. Lack is fear. The world is changing now from fear to love and it's so very beautiful. But that's for another time and perhaps another book.

Also, you can do the yoga "tree pose" for grounding or visualize yourself as a tree that is grounded with strong roots. When you are grounded, nothing can sway you and your branches because you are so rooted and connected to your intuition and yourself. Like a tree, you might bend a little when things get stormy, but you're not going to break. Your roots are stable and connected.

What happens "outside of you" doesn't "uproot" you because you are regulated within. Today, I practice grounding myself like this on a daily basis. I need it and I love it. It brings me so much peace and stability.

Getting grounded also means not asking everyone else what you should do, like I used to do. You will begin to trust your inner guidance. We all have it. Begin to create a deep relationship with yourself and trust the Universe is only guiding you for your "highest good." Trust your intuition rather than trying to get consensus outside of you from other people. You have all the answers. No one knows what's best for you than you and the Universe that's guiding you. You just need to get quiet and trust that you are being divinely guided and protected. Always, even when it doesn't feel that way. We just need to lean in to love and trust this. You will see remarkable results.

There are also many different kinds of breathing techniques available to help you relax or fall asleep. For example, try inhaling for four seconds, holding your breath for seven seconds, then exhaling for four seconds. That will bring you back into your body and reconnect with yourself. Another is to inhale and exhale for the same amount of time. In for four seconds, out for four seconds. Gradually, you can increase the amount of time you inhale and exhale. You can listen to guided breathing meditations for relaxation on one of the apps like Calm or Headspace.

Affirmations and practicing gratitude have literally saved my life. Every day, I say positive affirmations of everything I want to manifest and express gratitude for what I have. Look in the mirror and tell yourself, *I love me. I am a beautiful soul. I am enough just the way I am. Thank you for all my blessings. I'm so proud of you, gorgeous Erica.* Have faith and say these things every single day.

Find spiritual leaders you resonate with and read their books or watch/listen to their talks. Fill your social media feed with positive people who are not stuck in their own egos. Delete or mute anyone on social media who doesn't make you feel good. This has been one of the best things I've ever done for my mental health. This all affects your mind and emotional state. What you take in, including the news, is what you become and what you give out. Be careful and discerning with this. I particularly love the "old school" spiritual teachers like Louise Hay (especially her book *You Can Heal Your Life)*, Ekhart Tolle, and Wayne Dyer. Find whoever you resonate with and learn everything you can from them. It works if you work it, and they want their messages to come across.

I'm also a huge fan of the Emotional Freedom Technique (EFT). It's a way of tapping on different meridian points of the body to reduce emotional triggers, and I have found it to be life-changing in healing trauma and anxiety associated with it. Other people find yoga, sound baths, breathwork, and cold plunges helpful.

Whatever works, do. Explore and experiment and find out what speaks to your soul and feels good to you.

Panic attacks, like the ones I had after I gave birth to Chloe, can make you feel like you're losing your mind. If you suffer from anxiety, always remember to ground yourself and maybe look into some natural supplements. If needed, ask your doctor for prescription medication. I used to take Lexapro, but now I find I am doing really well supplementing with ashwagandha, L-theanine, liquid B-12, and vitex berry for hormone stabilization. Experiment and make sure to check in with your health provider if you have any questions or concerns.

There are many natural supplements out there. Listen to yourself and your body, do your own research, and find what's right for you.

If you're looking for support, different healing practitioners are there to help you on your journey: psychics, mediums, counselors, reiki practitioners, life coaches, chiropractors, acupuncturists, and cranial sacral therapists. I'm very grateful to have benefited greatly from amazing healers, and so can you.

If you're overwhelmed about where to start, my advice is to follow your intuition. It's never wrong. Let the Universe know you are ready and you will be given all the perfect resources. The teacher shows up when the student is ready. The more you start practicing self-care and self-love in the name of grounding yourself, the more automatic it becomes. The habit gets ingrained and starts to be second nature. I promise.

We all have to go through the difficult, "dark" stuff to reach the gorgeous, "juicy and light" stuff. And then perhaps back to the dark again. This is what healing looks like. You keep going deeper and deeper. Feeling it all, deeply loving yourself through it, and using grounding techniques like the ones I've outlined here is the way through the darkness and into the light in your life. Always remember, the more work you put into raising your vibration, the quicker you'll manifest everything you want in life. The "higher" your "vibration" and the more "aligned" you are with yourself, the quicker you will manifest all your heart's desires!

LESSON SIX

Boundaries = Safety for Everyone

The stress of interviewing for a spot in kindergarten in New York City like it was Harvard (such a silly thing) was the straw that broke the camel's back for me. It was very hard to get into one of the good public schools. New York is great, but living where it's cold and gray half the time was not making me happy or fulfilled. I definitely had SAD (seasonal affective disorder) in the winter. Many people thrive in Manhattan, but although I absolutely love visiting New York now, my journey there was coming to an end.

Still, I wasn't thinking seriously about leaving the city—I thought I was a tough, badass lifelong New Yorker!—until we went on a vacation in Florida. We were staying with Husband's parents in Boca Raton, and we went to have some alone time while they took care of the kids. It sounded like fun to have no responsibilities for a day or two, so we headed to South Beach. We were riding around on beach cruisers there when it hit me that the people there were really living. Like, *really* enjoying their lives, not just going through the motions.

Moms were playing with their kids in the ocean and hanging out with them at these cool playgrounds that seemed to be on every corner. The sun was shining so bright, and everyone was eating food that was fresh and healthy and easy to find. Meanwhile, I had just come from minus three degrees where I had to figure out how to carry groceries and push a double stroller through snow with crying kids in it at the same time. This looked like heaven on earth to me.

When things are meant to change and evolve, the Universe will make it happen, and that was it for me. I threw down my bike and said, "I'm done!"

Whenever my husband told this story after the fact, he'd always joke that he thought I meant I was done with *him*. (We were very happy together at the time, and honestly, it was foreshadowing, even though I didn't yet know that we would divorce years later.) At the time, what I meant was that I was done with New York. I hated the pressure and the weather and how the darkness made me depressed—even with the help of a little bit of Lexapro.

I followed up with, "Let's move here."

My husband thought I was nuts, but the idea started growing on him. When we got back, he looked for a new job in Florida and quickly landed a job as editor-in-chief at a popular South Florida magazine. Elated, I wrote a goodbye letter to New York that basically said, *I love you, but you're much too bright, loud, cold, and gray,* and that was that. I think I was also looking to leave behind all the trauma I experienced in NYC as well. We moved to Miami.

The way everything fell into place so easily—basically in one weekend—made me feel like it was absolutely meant to be. Everything was so divinely timed that I knew it was the right decision. I felt like the Universe was saying, *She's ready. She's been through enough here and learned enough for now. We're going to give her a little break and bring her to a magical place where she can finally slow down and discover her magical gifts.*

As the Universe would have it, Miami is called the Magic City, and our move was like magic to me. I always say my darkness turned to light (literally and figuratively) from the move from New York to Miami. I went from a rainy, cold, freezing, dark, dreary, stressful, and miserable place where I experienced a lot of my own darkness to one that was always bright, sunny, happy, gorgeous, warm, and delicious. Miami has a totally different vibration than New York. After living here for ten years now, I *still* can't believe I get to live in paradise every day and have so much deep gratitude that I get to call Miami my home.

I never want to trash Manhattan, though, because I love spending time there now. After healing my relationship with myself, I realize my problems were never New York's fault in the first place. We just had to break up for a while for me to realize the lack of boundaries I had while living there and the deep healing I've done since has helped me create a different relationship with the city, my first love and it's still my forever home.

That was such a turning point for me. I was now in a place where everyone was always in a good mood and knew how blessed they were. I was and remain beyond grateful today for my magical city and feeling so at home here.

My kids started school, and I immediately met a group of women from all over the world—Sweden, Brazil, Venezuela, Colombia, and more—who had all just moved to Miami, too. I always say I was greeted by a group of angels; they are so amazing. I know we all have had past life connections because our bond is so strong. It's like we were meant to start this journey together. So much has happened in all of our lives, but ten years later, we still come back home to each other and reconnect with so much beauty, support, and love.

I got recertified to practice psychotherapy in Florida and rented a space in Miami Beach to do therapy in and got back to work. I've always had a major interest in health, mindfulness, and wellness, so I took an online program to get an additional certification in holistic health and nutrition. I thought it would be great to combine my new skills with psychotherapy and that people in Miami would really respond to that. I loved it!

It all turned out to be part of my journey and calling. This led me to my purpose. The program taught me about meditation—and then the Universe taught me that when I meditated, I connected with Spirit (all energies in the spirit world—the Universe, angels, spirit guides, dead loved ones). That's how it all began for me: simple meditation. When you get still and quiet, you are able to connect, hear, and see so much other than the spiritual 3-D world most live in daily. So many people have a fear of this, so they never slow down or get quiet to let this energy in. They choose to block it out, and that's okay if that's what you need to do.

At first, I only felt and saw different energies that looked like blocks of light. Next, entities. Then messages. It was equal parts exciting and terrifying. The sensations I perceived were so strong.

I had no idea what was going on until a spiritual teacher told me that for the first time in my life, I was relaxed enough to be able to receive Spirit. I'd been brought to Miami (the "magic city") to discover my magic and to open up to my abilities so I could begin to heal myself and others.

One night, I woke up fearfully and physically felt energies coming at me—they were literally touching me. I was so scared and overwhelmed. It was a definite reflection of the fear I was feeling at the time. We attract what we energetically are and where we're at vibrationally. Another time, I was in the bathtub and started seeing scary apparitions. I now know I was connecting to a much lower, fear-based vibration because I was fearful of this at the time. Due to the lack of boundaries in my own life and my fear, I attracted this lower vibrational energy around me. Today, I'm super strong with my boundaries and dwell in the light and only see, feel, and connect with high-vibrational Spirit. Also due to my state and vibration now, I connect with a Spirit that is very light and funny. The Universe and Spirit has a great sense of humor, and if you're vibing in that vibration, you will see and feel it everywhere. I love it.

A bunch of other weird things started happening, too. I'd suddenly know something I couldn't possibly know without someone else—who wasn't living on this planet anymore—telling me. I tried my best to blow those off as just a coincidence, but after a while, I couldn't deny there was something big going on with me.

One time, I asked my husband, "What does Frogger mean to you?" He shot me a weird look. I told him, "Your mother is telling me about the Atari game she got you a million years ago." She then brought back a memory of his favorite "Frogger watch" that was a gift from her. There was no other way I could have known that—his mother died when he was a young boy, he and I didn't meet until we were eighteen, and he'd definitely never shared anything with me about his Frogger game.

And then this happened: I was doing therapy with a woman in my office when her dead brother suddenly appeared next to her. This was the first time I so clearly saw a person who had passed over. I knew he had died but not how, and now I could literally see that he'd shot himself in the head. (I've since asked Spirit not to show me some of these gruesome visuals, and they respect my boundaries.) Even though he looked like he was in really bad shape, he was communicating, *Everything's okay. It wasn't her fault. Please tell her she couldn't have done anything to stop it.* He kept reiterating that to me.

It was so intense physically for me and for the first time in fifteen years as a therapist, I had to excuse myself and leave the room during a therapy session. I felt nauseous. I was convinced I was having a nervous breakdown. I splashed water on my face in the bathroom and tried to breathe, hoping this wasn't going to turn into a full-blown panic attack. When I went back into my office, the brother was gone. I tried to act normal and continue the session, the same as always. It wasn't easy, but somehow I did it.

I was terrified I was going crazy, but Nora and Alex (my best friends in Miami at the time) kept reassuring me that I was connecting to the other side and not to be afraid of my abilities. They knew so much more about this and said the information I was receiving wasn't happening to make me feel insane—it was happening because I was supposed to share my gift and help heal lots of people. They'd seen psychics and had abilities themselves, so they were able to recognize that I did, too. They were much more familiar with this world than me, so I was so grateful to have them. They helped me so much during this time and are still such bright lights in my life and always will be.

After that, the Universe, with humor, confirmed their assurances to me. I started seeing the word "medium" everywhere I went. I saw that our large moving boxes Husband had brought home had "medium" written on them in huge letters. I never saw that written on a box. I went to a makeup store where I had always bought a lighter shade before, but now it didn't look right. When I mentioned the tone looked off to the salesperson, she explained they'd switched all the branding and said to me, "You're a medium!" I laughed to myself, and I was just beginning to see that the Universe is always talking to us through signs, synchronicities, and people. The same thing happened in a clothing store. I said, "I'm always a size small here." I certainly hadn't put on any weight, but the person working there still looked at me and said, "No, you're a medium." The Universe was being funny!

Now this happens most days, but it's very subtle because I can control the energy now. I'm so used to it and love it, but back then, this was just the beginning and I thought it was so wild. I told my friends, and they thought it was amazing and hysterical.

Soon after that, I went to a magazine work event with my husband. I didn't want to because at this time, I was just learning about my gifts and my boundaries weren't so good and dead people kept trying to talk to me everywhere I went. I didn't know how to tune them out, but something forced me to go. I now know it was Spirit and my intuition giving me that nudge.

As soon as I walked into this crazy party in South Beach, everyone's dead friends and relatives started competing for my attention just like I knew they would. I didn't want to deal with their energy, but I still didn't have boundaries in place to know how to block them out. I started to have trouble breathing and was feeling really overwhelmed, so I went to sit in the bar by myself.

I was drinking a glass of white wine and trying to avoid the Spirits when a model whom my husband knew came over. I thought, *Oh, I have no desire to talk to anyone right now,* but then she sat down and we talked about lots of cool, spiritual stuff. I liked her. She later became my friend Kasey. She told me, "You would love my psychic mentor Nicola in LA. You should call her."

She truly saved my life with that referral. (This is why we have to go wherever we're feeling pushed to because the Universe is telling us something even if it doesn't make sense in our logical minds.) I called Nicola the next day, and she meditated with me, did an energy healing, and confirmed that I was a spiritual healer and a medium. She helped me ground my energy and begin to understand how to use my gifts. She isn't a medium herself, but she is intuitive and understands all of this work. Through her, I learned about boundaries, compassionate detachment, and balancing my spiritual gifts all while living a normal life—whatever that is! We've also worked a lot on healing my personal trauma as well.

Nicola opened an exciting and magical new world to me. She got it, and I felt safe with my new abilities now. I started to calm down and enjoy my purpose and mission. I became obsessed with how much I could help people heal. Soon, I thought every part of this new spiritual journey was fascinating and couldn't get enough of it.

The more I worked with Nicola, the more I was able to tap into the love and light. As I continued to practice meditation, listening, and focusing, my energy started to shift. I was connecting to a much higher vibe. Now I only connect to the spiritual world with positivity and love, which really helps the people I work with.

Once again, the Universe had guided me to exactly where I needed to be. I didn't want to go to that party, but something told me I needed to be there. Don't force yourself to go where it doesn't feel right. Get quiet and listen to your inner guidance; it knows you what to do.

I quickly transitioned from doing traditional therapy to spiritual readings and healings. I'm not sure exactly how it happened (that was Spirit's job), but it all fell into place beautifully. Pretty soon, I knew it was time to "come out of the spiritual closet" to other important people in my life. Of course I was worried about what they'd think about it and assumed they'd judge me.

It's funny how I've come so full circle with this. I don't care at all what anyone thinks anymore, so no one cares either about what I do. That's how it goes. When you decide to embrace your authentic truth rather than fear it, something far better always happens.

You express your truest passion and purpose, people identify with that, and all the fear and worry goes away. Also, people are so focused on themselves that they don't have much time to care about what anyone else is doing. If you feel good about you, it shines through, and that's all that matters. Remember, all is well beyond the fear, and beyond the fear, all is well.

I started by telling my dad first. We were in a health food restaurant in Miami, and I was so nervous that my heart was pounding. I explained what had been happening with me, and in his thick Brooklyn accent, he just said, "You're a what?" He had no idea what a medium is. After I explained it, he said, "Maybe I believe in all that stuff, too, baby. I talk to your mom every day. She doesn't talk much back, but I know she hears me." Since then, there have been many times I've channeled my mom by myself and with my dad, sharing comforting and healing messages from her to him.

Once my dad saw me having success in the spiritual world and thriving as an entrepreneur, he began to think it was cool. He was happy for me and proud that I am living my passion and helping people heal.

A lot of people in my family have psychic abilities and we never knew—my grandma, mom, sister, and cousin—and I started thinking, *Hmm, maybe my dad does, too.* He's definitely very intuitive and empathic. I never thought of him as psychic before, but maybe he just uses his abilities differently, like many other people do. Many of you are reading people and energy all of the time but don't know it.

Last year, I was out with my dad and his amazing friend. His dead son came through to me, and it was such a magical moment when I told him he was there. He had a lot of intimate things to say, and he cried and felt so light and relieved after. My dad was stunned to witness him validate my words. I also gave my dad messages from my mom that night. She made a lot of jokes. They both loved it. It was a special dinner.

Recently in Miami, I was out to dinner with my dad and my younger daughter, and we wanted to figure out how my mom's dad had died. It was a mystery that no one knew. Lola was talking, and I was like, "Hold on one second, I'm trying to talk to your dead great-grandpa! Let me see what this man is going to tell us." She just said, "Oh, okay, Mom, I'll be quiet so you can talk to him," and we all laughed. Even my dad thought it was totally normal, yet comical.

Honestly, I'm not such a woo-woo person. I mean, I love my crystals, oils, sage, and such just as much as the next healer, but I'm also fully present and grounded in the real world. I have kids and a real-world life and I have to be. I'm the first person to make jokes about how crazy this stuff is, but it is also so very beautiful and real.

Soon, I began to tell other people in my life. Some who had known me forever thought it was nuts and had no idea how to react. I'm just Erica to them, and it still doesn't come up when we're together. Sometimes that's very relaxing to me to be with people who knew me before these abilities and who don't really care at all. For people who are new in my life, it's one of the most frequent topics we talk about because it's a big part of my identity now, and I've attracted people on my vibration who are in the spiritual world like me and very interested in this work.

A few months after I discovered my healing abilities, I was on the phone doing a spiritual coaching session with a client who was struggling because her mother had cancer, was hospitalized, and in a coma. As we continued to speak, I began to receive messages from her mom. I heard apologies for how she'd treated my client. She described exactly what my client was wearing at that moment—this was a voice call, and I was in Miami while she was in California, so I certainly had no idea what she was wearing—and that she'd just gotten a specific brand of granola bar from the vending machine. *How was this woman communicating with me?* I wondered. She was alive! I shared this with my client, and all of it was true. Needless to say, we were both blown away.

Since then, I've worked with clients in comas as well as people who are nonverbal to help their loved ones communicate with them. I recently was in a home where a man was in a coma (in between the spiritual and earthly world), and I saw that his dead relatives had come to greet him. I telepathically let him know it was okay to go with them, and he died peacefully a day later. This ability to communicate with nonverbal people is just another magical gift for which to be thankful. It's all just "energy" no matter what form it's in, and I read it and connect and chat with it.

In Miami, I felt like everything in my life just clicked into place. It is my perfect home. I made great friends almost immediately (my angel sisters for life). I started building a business that is now thriving beyond my wildest dreams. I manifested all of this, and I couldn't be happier.

All of us have different ideas of our own dream life. This is my dream life. I get to live my passion in a gorgeous, sunny place surrounded by people I love and who love me back. I could not ask for anything more.

My light broke the darkness that had followed me for so long. And if I made that happen for myself, so can you.

WHAT I NOW KNOW

Once I learned how to connect to a higher vibe and protect my boundaries, I really came to love helping people communicate with their loved ones, angels, and spiritual guides, and cleansing their energy and providing them with guidance to truly heal whatever is blocking the life of their dreams.

I've also learned that the more boundaries you have on earth, the more boundaries you have with the spirit world. A doctor doesn't want to perform surgery at a party or when picking their kid up from school or when they're trying to sleep, and it's the same idea for me. These days, Spirits rarely bug me when I'm not trying to connect with them, but if they do, I just tell them, *Not now,* and they get it. Or if I feel the urgency for a reason, I'll entertain it. This has come with years of practice creating my own boundaries in the earthly plane. It always blows me away when people who are fearful of this work tell mediums to leave the dead alone. I don't know one medium who has ever sought out to bother the dead; it's definitely the other way around. They get so excited when they see a medium that they try to get through all of the time. You don't realize how many spirits there are everywhere. Everyone you see has so many around them that they knew in this life or past lives trying to get messages through, and as a medium, it's our job to have strong boundaries so we don't go insane. I'm still telling them to stop on a daily basis and to find a way to connect me with their living relative to book a session, and when I do, the Universe makes it magically happen.

Boundaries take a lot of work, but they're so worth it. We need to protect our physical and emotional energy always. I get to say who, what, and when anything can enter my space, and so do you! My job and yours is to take care of and focus on ourselves and our growth.

As an empath, I tended to take on everyone else's pain and suffering and forget my own. Many of you who were drawn to read this book are the same. I learned that to be physically and emotionally okay, I simply can't do that to myself anymore. Don't do that to yourself anymore either. It only leads to anger, resentment, exhaustion, depression, anxiety, and a whole slew of health problems that come from all the stress. When that happens, you are no good for yourself or anyone else.

Whenever you're feeling some intense energy out of the blue, take a deep breath and ask yourself, *Is this mine or someone else's? Or is it just that the world is so heavy and intense right now? Or did I just start to feel this way right after meeting with this particular person?* This helps determine where the energy is coming from and whom it belongs to. Yes, it takes time and practice, but keep at it.

I now believe a big percentage of my depression and anxiety growing up was not my own but my sensitivity to absorbing all of the energy of others around me. I didn't know how to have boundaries and differentiate the two back then. I just have to remind myself that everything happens at the time it's supposed to happen for us to grow and evolve.

Knowing when feelings belong to someone else can literally change your life dramatically. When you know they are not yours, energetically send them off. Visualize yourself in a bright white bubble of light that allows you to keep your energy to yourself, or visualize mirrors facing outward are covering you and deflecting anyone else's energy. You can also burn sage and palo santo to clear people's energy off your aura. I almost always sage my house after people have left.

Affirmations work, too. Try, *I feel so peaceful and calm in my own energy and I do not take on the negative energy of others.* If that doesn't feel right for you, make up something else that resonates more.

Many crystals, such as smoky quartz and black obsidian, also work for energy protection. You can wear those as jewelry or simply carry the rocks with you when you know the energy is going to get intense. When I was particularly sensitive, I used to wear crystals in my bra (not so uncommon with women who do what I do) to absorb the harsh energy around me. And once, when I was at the airport (heavy energy there), they made the X-ray machine go off. There were a lot of laughs over that, and I was quite embarrassed.

Today's generation is more self-aware and spiritually evolved. Most of them came here knowing things that took older generations years to get or never got at all. Teach them boundaries early. Explain to your kids that sometimes what they are feeling is coming from someone else, not from inside of themselves. Talk about how if a person, place, or thing doesn't feel right to them, it's not by accident. They are feeling this for a reason, and their intuition is telling them something's wrong and they don't have to doubt themselves.

Chances are, if you picked up this book, you're an empath and need to start working on your boundaries and protecting your energy. Knowing where you end and other people begin is so important. No is a full sentence! If we're bled dry of all our energy, we're not good for ourselves or anyone else. We get exhausted. We get sick. We get angry and misaligned (not in the flow of our higher selves and who we really are).

In the end, the only people you are responsible for are your minor children and *you*. You are not responsible for your parents, husband, wife, boyfriend, girlfriend, boss, coworkers, strangers, or best friend. They have themselves and the Universe to connect with as their source of love, energy, and peace. Love comes from within us, not from another person on the outside. Of course we can love each other, but we are not each other's "source" of love. Don't give away your energy to other people at the expense of you. I learned from my amazing coach Cristina that "leaking" your energy or "taking" from you to help others is not in alignment with source, the Universe, or the highest good of anyone. Loving you fully and setting boundaries lights you up in a way that lights up the people around you. You come first and then you can "harmonize" with others.

And if people don't like the new boundaries you start putting in place, that's okay. Do you. They're probably the ones who need them most and they will learn from you and you will begin to feel powerful and fabulous.

LESSON SEVEN

Always Keep Growing and Healing

One night (when I was a teenager) after I'd become aware of different ways of expressing sexuality, I asked my mom how she would feel if I told her I was gay. It was a way different time than it is now; I was curious about my mom's reaction. She immediately responded, "Why the fuck would I care?" Haha, she was a badass, too. She really modeled being open-minded and accepting for me, which is probably why I'm able to relate to my children in the same way today. Whoever they are and whatever they want to be is my dream for them. Be you. Do you. This is *your* life, not a dress rehearsal and no one else's. The world would be in a lot better shape if we all loved ourselves more and accepted others for who they are. This has been a recent lesson of mine and it's really had wonderful results.

Just as my mom's example helped me grow emotionally and feel safe to be me in some ways, once I discovered my abilities, I found myself soaring in incredible new directions spiritually. I was constantly opening up and moving forward. My new way of being in the world represented the full truth of who I am and my purpose for this lifetime.

I believe in following your bliss and freedom and making the right choices to be happy. Having discovered this magical new way of living, there was no way I could deny my newfound self. I knew I could live the life of my wildest dreams and wasn't going to waste a second more not living it! I wanted more and more freedom and growth! I wanted to soar as high as possible!

Unfortunately, Husband and I weren't on the same page with this stuff. I think my new abilities, interests, and direction were very intense for him. Now I see that clearly. This super spiritual journey isn't for everyone, and that's okay. Everyone does not choose this level of evolvement in the same lifetime. We were very young when we got together, and I was a different person then; you either grow together or you grow apart, and that's okay. Everyone should find their peace and their bliss at whatever time in their lives. Our society is very fearful in this way, judging people for not staying together for life. That feels so archaic and codependent to me. But the new generations are catching on to this. They get it. They just want to be free and at peace, no matter what that looks like. I think that's amazing. We were simply learning and growing in different directions. I want my girls to always do what feels joyful and peaceful to them in relationships and in life.

Eventually, it was time to separate and divorce. This was definitely not an easy thing, but life is not supposed to be easy. It was, however, absolutely necessary for us to both move forward with our lives.

When any relationship ends, whether romantic or platonic, it means the lessons both parties need to learn from the other have been learned. The "soul contract is complete." On a spiritual level, no one has failed; it's just "done." It's simply time to move on separately and grow in different ways.

Although there is 50-50 responsibility for what happens throughout the course of any relationship, the end is always the hardest to navigate. Despite the grief and sadness, though, the ending of a soul contract, in time, can lead to very positive things. It allows both parties to move on in freedom and authenticity rather than living a codependent lie (like way too many people are currently doing) to please each other or portray a certain picture to the world. Yes, everyone has to deal with the consequences their decisions have on the other individuals involved, but following your heart is always worth it, and in the end, your children and people around you will benefit from it. Any one decision made out of love and following your heart is the right one and will ultimately work out for the "highest good" for all involved. Stagnancy doesn't help anyone grow, heal, and learn.

It was a very difficult, traumatic, and trying time after our divorce and some of my hardest lessons ever learned, but I know everything is always meant to be as it is. I'm still learning and growing and healing from this experience, and that's okay. We need to follow our hearts and intuition, *always*.

Much of my new growth has been spurred by deep inner-child healing work with my spiritual coach. I'm beyond grateful to the healers and my mentor who have worked with me to help me give me the love I was missing from myself and my lack of connection to the Universe and Source. Deeply healing my inner child and learning my love comes from the Universe (Source, God, Divinity—whatever word you like) and me, not other people, has helped me beyond measure to be in such a happy, peaceful, safe, and grounded place today, loving myself beyond. I learned through this work that loving myself means paying attention to me and my needs. Unfortunately, we all too often forget to do this.

I've done a ton of work to heal and process the emotional neglect and abandonment I experienced in my past, which left me with a burning internal rage (really covering up my deep sadness and loneliness) thus seeking "love" outside of me. It's easier for most of us to be angry instead of sad and vulnerable. When that rage was expressed in words, it was scary and I've since learned I didn't know how to control myself. I was scared of myself as well and unleashing that anger on others. It's a result of unprocessed and unhealed trauma. We store it in our brains and body. That's why releasing it physically and mentally is so important. You can begin to notice this in people in your life who behave this way. They are deeply suffering and in pain. Thus the saying "Hurt people hurt people." Of course you shouldn't accept any abuse, but to know that you or someone you know is acting this way possibly due to trauma will help. So if needed, encourage you to get the help you need (different professionals and healing modalities that feel right to you, like discussed earlier in the book, can help) and try to encourage your loved ones who have experienced trauma to as well.

Healing my inner-child rage has deeply helped my communication skills and I am able to express myself without becoming aggressive and going on the attack. I'm able to be strong and assertive in a loving way now. I'm not perfect and I'm still a human and I have my slips, but the positive effect this work has had on my relationships is mindblowing. I've regulated my nervous system, which was out of whack and dysregulated for so long.

A recent example: Before I did my inner-child healing, I got very aggressive and annoyed on a date because the guy didn't want to go where I wanted to go and disagreed with a lot of my opinions. As a result, he told me, "I don't like your energy or want to spend time with you." Wow. Thank you, Universe, for this man giving me this lesson! After I did my inner work, I texted him thanking him for pointing out some things I needed to improve on in my way of relating to others. He was kind and understood, and it felt like a nice healing moment for us both.

We are all mirrors for each other, helping each other grow and evolve.

Since my healing, I've forgiven everyone whom I used to feel harmed by but really see now that they were just mirrors of me, causing me to become my highest self.

Most importantly, I forgave me. That's the only way you can heal and see the lesson and forgive others. We are all just doing the best we could with the conscious tools and skills we have.

This is a hard one to grasp, but I am totally responsible (and so are you) for what we attract into our lives and how we choose to respond to it. I own that responsibility now and it is extremely powerful, loving, and healing. We create (through our thoughts, energy, and vibration) all that shows up in our life. Yes, *everything*. Many people will dislike me or be very triggered by reading this, and that's okay. This is purely the law of attraction. We learn and our souls grow from these experiences. This might be hard to comprehend, but when you get to a level where you can clearly see and accept this, true deep gorgeous freedom lies. It is very empowering and the complete opposite of being in victim mentality, I promise you. We manifest all that shows up in our lives, *always*.

My anger and aggression grew out of a need for self-protection. I've since learned that I hadn't felt safe in the world (common for people who've experienced trauma) like I do now. No one was there to protect me when I needed it, so I took on a very masculine energy as well. It lived in me for so long that I lost touch with my feminine side and presented myself to the world as an alpha female. So many women do this and are perceived as aggressive "bitches." They are just protecting themselves and wearing "armor" so they don't get hurt again. That was me, and many men experience this as well.

Now that I've worked through my childhood wounds, my masculine and feminine divine are well-balanced. I know I can be assertive, competent, and a badass boss and still have a soft, vulnerable gorgeous flowing feminine side as well.

The bottom line: Where you're at internally is what you manifest externally.

WHAT I NOW KNOW

There's a lot of letting go and surrendering in realizing we cannot control and do not own anybody—not our partners, friends, parents, or kids. Am I perfect at this? Definitely not. Am I learning, growing and getting better every day? I want other people to figure this out as well and soar and have a sense of freedom to manifest the life of their own dreams.

My experience has also made me see relationships between children and parents so differently. There are many parents who are extremely codependent with their children (I was guilty of this for some time). This is a common theme among the women I know and clients of mine. They look to their kids to give them a life and a purpose, but the truth is, we all need to find that on our own. We brought these amazing humans into the world to thrive in their own lives and learn from their own mistakes, not to give us our happiness. That is way too much pressure on these kids (I see it everyday), and we are responsible to make our own happiness. This goes the same for so many other relationships in our lives. We are all whole just the way we are and don't need anyone else to complete us.

I was at the gym the other day and a woman was saying how she was happy that her college-aged daughter was home for a visit but was so beyond devastated that she only "got" her for three days. Of course as a mom, I can relate to the emotions that come up when our kids become less dependent on us. I also wished for the mom to focus on making her own life more fulfilling outside of her role as a mother (find her own passion that sets her soul on fire) and have more gratitude that her daughter is thriving as a young adult out there on her own.

We need to set our children free and love ourselves so they can do the same for themselves. It's a hard lesson, to be sure, but it's such an important one.

I want more than anything for my children to be free and independent and love how special and fabulous they are. I want them to live their own lives and their own truth. I'm always here for love, guidance, comfort, support, and fun, but I am not trying to control them or make them feel like they owe me anything. This isn't about me—it's about them doing what lights them up and makes them realize their purpose here on earth.

This leads me to the biggest lesson of all: *your life is your own.* You can make anything you want of it. Don't let others tell you who you should be or what you should do. You don't owe anyone any explanation. You have the choice to decide what you want, when you want all the time.

So follow your own intuition. It is your guide. Know that when something feels off to you, that's because it is. Challenge everyone and everything that feels "misaligned" with you. Forge your own path. Do not put anyone else on a pedestal above you. They are as confused and lost as everyone else on this journey of trying to figure it all out. Only you and the Universe know what's for your highest good.

The world is changing so fast and upgrading our energy frequency. Don't give in to fear. Focus on love and open your heart. Open your throat chakra, speak up for yourself, and allow your voice and truth to be heard—not only for those who are asleep but for your own healing.

The Universe is always watching. The more good you put into the world, the more good comes back to you. Karma is real. If you make a mistake and slip a little, don't beat yourself up over it. You are enough. Always. More than enough. Do the work and find the tools—start by using the ones found in this book—to love yourself back into alignment with your truth.

Remember, you attract what you put out in the world. Keep your goals in mind and continually strive to rise higher. Dream big. Do good. Put you first and love you.

Let light and love lead the way. It's all karma. Everything works out exactly the way it's supposed to. As my dad always said, this too shall pass. And "it" did.

LESSON EIGHT

Self-Love Is the Answer

To be able to love and accept others, we first need to truly love and accept ourselves. Through lots of healing work, I learned to put myself first because no one else was going to, and that's the only way I feel okay, grounded, and happy. Otherwise, I would be a scattered mess, like I was in the past. Self-love is the least "selfish" thing you can do. It's a gift to you and everyone else.

I now try to show what being a loving, accepting, happy, and fulfilled woman is to my daughters and hope they know how truly special and beautiful and unique and powerful they are. I also teach self-love to my clients all around the world. Self-love is "paying attention" to you and your needs and taking care of them and putting them first. I believe self-care is key in life, and self-love can help heal the world.

My self-care routine includes making sure I get as much sleep as my body needs and drinking tons of water. I listen to my body when it tells me to stop eating and drinking (when you clean out your system and your hormones are balanced, you will know what your body needs). My body talks to me, and so will yours. I get outside and connect with nature as much as possible. This grounds and calms my nervous system. I only allow loving, supportive people into my life. I am supported by amazing professionals in the areas I need it. I follow my passion and purpose in life. And having major boundaries is of course part of my self-care and self-love routine. I come first, and my needs matter so much; yours do, too.

These things above are a great way to start on your journey to self-love. My most recent inner-child healing work has taken self-love to a much deeper level, as we can always be going deeper and deeper into our growth healing. This involves deep inner-child "mirror work" with my spiritual coach Cristina to deeply feel all of my feelings (something most of us haven't done for our whole lives), let them come out to the surface to be felt and expressed, release them, and send myself love and whatever else I need to feel peace and safety and expansiveness. We do this with the "mirror exercise." The concept behind it is that we are all just mirroring and triggering each other into looking at and healing what we need to heal in ourselves. Whatever someone triggers in you just points to a part of you that needs deep love and healing. They are actually giving you a gift to look at yourself and feel and release and love what's triggering you. This is very deep, intense, and difficult (at times) work, but the rewards are miraculous and magical. I'm grateful every day for it.

Another part of self-care and self-love includes having a full and fulfilling sexual life. Sex is such a huge part of our lives, but it often gets ignored. I know it does for many others I work with, and it did for me in the past as well. After my divorce, I realized I am a very sexual being (most of us are) and I needed to explore that part of me often.

I believe to thrive at your utmost potential, those human physical needs have to be addressed and fulfilled. Good sex has a ton of health benefits, from better sleep to better mental health. It literally enhances your physical appearance. Orgasms (with yourself or others) make you glow because they hold such sacred, intense, awesome, beautiful energy. They calm you down and are so good for your mental health as well.

Sexuality, sensuality, and spirituality are a whole new calling for me these days. Now I get to have those experiences, and it's so delicious. I feel ageless and alive, and it's amazing. (We are all ageless, by the way. I feel like I've been aging backward since my spiritual journey began as many on this path do. This is due to all the high-vibe spiritual life force energy. How you feel is what matters, and when you begin to do this work and get in this mindset, you will look and feel ageless, too!)

The more I opened up about my sexual rebirth to my friends and clients, the more they were able to begin exploring their hidden desires as well. We love talking about it all. Spiritual individuals who love themselves are very sexual and are having a blast exploring it all, and so should you if you so choose. There are no inhibitions when you are in this energetic space, and it's amazing. Being your authentic self, especially sexually, has so many rewards.

Connecting, loving, touching, intimacy, merging—sex encompasses all that is beautiful in life. It is a gift to be savored and enjoyed. Humans need it to survive and thrive. Accept and receive it wholly and fully.

WHAT I NOW KNOW

Toward the end of my sessions, I usually get a final message from Spirit. Most of the time, it's, *Remember, you come first.* This is because there is such a lack of self-love on this planet. You come first because you are so important. Self-sacrificing for others is not following your soul's purpose. Your purpose is to light yourself up. By doing this, your light will guide others out of their darkness.

So many people, especially women, feel they don't deserve self-care or that they should come last. That's absolutely not the case. For you to light up and feel good and to be in service of others, you first have to serve yourself.

I recently worked with a woman in her fifties who thought she was too old to figure out her purpose and passion. Her dead grandma came through to tell her, "That's rubbish! It's never too late!" (The rubbish part made her laugh—the specific phrases are how people know it's really their relatives.) This British grandmother's words helped the woman realize that she'd spent her whole life taking care of everyone else, and now it was her turn. She then felt validated and motivated to do so.

Self-care and self-love extend to caring for the sexual side of yourself. Living your best life means being balanced in all aspects of it. Obviously, do the best you can to fulfill all areas of your life. When you're having an active, amazing, thriving sexual life, you're thriving everywhere else and vice versa. The way you do one thing is the way you do everything. And there are many spiritual teachers who believe and teach that if you think of what you want to manifest in your life while having an orgasm, it will come to fruition.

There's so much guilt and shame around pleasure—it doesn't even have to be sexually. We all need, want, and deserve pleasure in our lives in all forms and we should have it. This isn't a dress rehearsal; it's your one and only magical life as you. Be whatever you want, no matter your age. You're worth it and you deserve it!

CONCLUSION

I told you at the start of this book that *all is well* (and can also be beyond magical) and I hope that you can see through my story that it is.

I certainly never "consciously" as a human asked to lose my mom at seventeen, to have an extremely emotionally abusive relationship with my stepmother, to lose contact with my sister for so many years now, to witness 9/11 and a suicide a few days later, to have crippling postpartum depression and anxiety, to be date raped and other very scary sexual experiences with men, to be violently mugged, to go through a very difficult divorce, or to endure through any of the many other difficult things I've since endured along the way. I see so clearly now that they were all parts of my journey I'd chosen as a soul before I got here to heal and learn and grow and live out my passion of helping others heal. I wouldn't change any of it. I'm not a victim, and neither are you. In retrospect, I chose my life's experiences without knowing it when I arrived as a human so that I could learn the lessons I needed to grow my soul, to teach others, and to heal within and without. Long before I knew the purpose of my life, I was manifesting a magical existence for myself. But first, I had to deal with a lot of difficult stuff. We all choose our path before we come here, and as we heal and come into "alignment" with who we are, we are able to choose more "feel good" experiences, as we are meant to "feel good." I just had to learn through some not-such-feel-good stuff first as many of you do as well.

Today, I am a happy mom to the two coolest humans I've ever met. I have the most supportive best friendships that I could imagine (focused on quality, not quantity), and I've healed through some very hard stuff and am very happy in my love life. I do whatever I want, whenever I want. I'm at peace and feel very peaceful and happy in it all. I have a thriving business working with clients from around the world, including both living and dead celebrities. I love me and am proud to be a psychic medium, spiritual advisor and healer, and holder of sacred space for others to heal. There's nowhere I'd rather be than playing around and experiencing in beautiful heavenly Miami, serving others with these gifts. I'm deeply grateful and feel immensely blessed for who I am and how far I've come. I'm so grateful, as all of the intense healing work has really paid off. Of course I am continuing to heal, grow, and learn every day as we all are. I wish for you to do the healing work to manifest the life of your dreams!

Please remember these lessons: (1) Your loved ones in spirit don't care about the drama—they just want you to be okay. (2) Everything happens according to the divine timing of the Universe. (3) What's calling you and lights you up is your purpose and passion in this life. (4) Helping others helps you. (5) Grounding is everything. (6) Boundaries are safety for everyone. (7) Always keep learning and growing. (8) Self-love is always the answer. (9) Always trust your inner guidance; it knows the way.

I know it's hard in your darkest moments to transcend trauma, pain, and loss. I've been there myself. The only thing that works is having unrelenting trust in the Universe (it's your bestie, always guiding you) and then trusting yourself and seeking out professional help when/if you're called to. You cannot do it all alone and do not have to. Healing comes first and that's how you are led to manifest the life of your dreams. You have to make the "space" for the abundance to "flow." Whatever you want is yours to manifest.

Nothing brings me greater satisfaction than the healing that comes through the spiritual and then shows up in the physical (it's all an inner journey), and I hope these pages have helped you understand you are a spiritual being with a divine purpose and a magical destiny and you deserve all that your heart desires and then some! I would love to hear about your journey from the darkness to the light. To connect with me, visit my website www.ericakorman.com and Instagram (@ericakorman).

Love and forgive and have compassion for you, and go out and live your life knowing you're exactly where you're meant to be, you have the power to get where you want to go, and no matter what is happening, all is well. In fact, all is beyond magical!

Love you,
Erica

ACKNOWLEDGMENTS

Thank you to my parents, Manny and Cora, and my daughters, Chloe and Lola, for being exactly who you are. (See book dedication to them in the front of the book!)

Thank you, my dearest friend and sister, Jay Jiggins, for literally "saving my life" in a few of my darkest moments. I will never ever forget the depth of your love, support, and friendship to me during such a difficult time and always. You are my sister. You're such a beautiful gift to this world and I love you (and your angel daughters) deeply and am forever grateful to you.

Thank you to my aunt Gail and cousin Kim for always being there and loving me so much and being my supporters and biggest fans throughout it all (even when you might have thought I was nuts). And to my uncle John and cousins Mike and Eileen for loving me and being my family. Thank you.

Thanks to my badass cousins Allison and Alan for being such fucking cool, strong survivors. Allison, I'm amazed at how far you've come in this life. Wow. Alan, you are a rock star warrior. You supported me and guided me (with the best humor) through some pretty hard shit. I look up to and admire you both so much and you each need to write your own book about your lives and resilience and what you've overcome. You guys have turned so much of our generational trauma into love and are the best parents ever. I love you and your families.

Thank you to my beautiful sister Meredith for being you. I love you always.

And to my wild bestie and "warrior in crime" Gia Languasco. OMG, I have no words for how deep my love and sisterhood is for you. Our connection is so rare and beautiful, and I love you beyond words. We have so much more fun and life to do together. Thank you for always "showing up" and loving and supporting me no matter what.

Thank you, my girl Jess Eliav, for always "getting me". Your warmth, depth, and authenticity are such a gorgeous asset to this planet. Our connection and friendship heals my heart and soothes my soul. You're so gorgeous. I love you and you have my heart.

Thanks to my other closest "angel" Miami sisters—Nora, Keanna, Alex, Monica, Ana, Jay, Vanessa, Paula, Marcy, Marisa, Sam, Claudia, and more not named. You guys are all so beyond special to me and celebrating and supporting each other through this life is a blast. I'm so blessed for your friendships, so excited for our future memories. I love and cherish you guys beyond.

And to my special buddy Jonathan Hofman, you are the brother I've never had and I've always wanted; you are a true "earth angel" and our friendship means the world to me. You have gently "held space" for all of my shit, and your positive way of seeing the world is so beautifully inspiring. Thank you for all of the support you have given me in so many areas of my life over the past years. My appreciation and gratitude run *muy* deep! Haha. Besos!

To my lifelong childhood sisters Sabrina and Caron, we have been together through it all. Wow, soo many years and so much life. Hard to say in words how deep my love is for you guys. You're both so real and so good and mean so much to me. Thank you, thank you, thank you.

And to my current and past therapist, mentors, and healers—Frima Christoper, Nicola Salter, Rev. Adriana LoveDriven, Ricardo Kmentt, and Cristina Fernandez—I wouldn't be here today and functioning like a somewhat "sane" (haha), stable, self-sufficient, regulated human without you guys. You guys "hold space" daily for such deep stuff with everyone you help and you are all pure love. I "see" you and all you do. Thank you.

Thank you to everyone at Scribe whom I worked with: Trish, Bianca, Kathleen, Annette, Mikey, Ploy, Jessica, Joyce, Caroline, and everyone else involved. You guys are amazing and it was a really great experience.

To Danielle Pisano, I know by the time this book comes out we will have manifested some super-big magic together! I see it. Thanks for your drive, ambition, and belief in my work. Yay!

And thanks to my ex-husband for all of the years of friendship, amazing memories, creating our beautiful girls together, and the dedication you have to them.

And to the men I dated post-divorce, I'm so grateful for all of the experiences, lessons, and friendships, some hard and some so beautifully healing to my heart and soul. I appreciate you.

A deepest thank-you to my beautiful clients (alive and dead). I'm still blown away daily by this work and meeting your loved ones in spirit. They are all so beautiful and I feel a deep connection to you all. It's an honor to work with you and I'm so grateful to be a part of your healing process. Love you all.

And thank you for reading this book and my story. I hope it helps you on your healing journey.

I love you and I'm beyond blessed. Thank you, thank you, thank you.